MACMILLAN READERS
INTERMEDIATE LEVEL

ÉMILE ZOLA

Thérèse Raquin

Retold by Elizabeth Walker

MACMILLAN

MACMILLAN READERS

INTERMEDIATE LEVEL

Founding Editor: John Milne

The Macmillan Readers provide a choice of enjoyable reading materials for learners of English. The series is published at six levels – Starter, Beginner, Elementary, Pre-intermediate, Intermediate and Upper.

Level control
Information, structure and vocabulary are controlled to suit the students' ability at each level.

The number of words at each level:

Starter	about 300 basic words
Beginner	about 600 basic words
Elementary	about 1100 basic words
Pre-intermediate	about 1400 basic words
Intermediate	about 1600 basic words
Upper	about 2200 basic words

Vocabulary
Some difficult words and phrases in this book are important for understanding the story. Some of these words are explained in the story and some are shown in the pictures. From Pre-intermediate level upwards, words are marked with a number like this: ...³. These words are explained in the Glossary at the end of the book.

Answer keys
Answer keys for the *Points for Understanding* and the *Exercises* sections can be found at www.macmillanenglish.com

A38707

Contents

A Note About the Author and France in the Nineteenth Century

Émile Zola was born in Paris on 2nd April 1840. His father, Francesco Zola, was Italian and his mother, Françoise-Émilie Aubert, was French. When Émile was three years old, the Zola family moved to Aix-en-Provence in southeastern France. Émile's father died four years later and the family became poor.

Émile Zola started school in the year that Louis Philippe, the King of France (1830–1848), was removed from the throne and the period called the Second Republic began. In 1852, Zola went to the Collège Bourbon in Aix-en-Provence. While he was there, he met Paul Cézanne, who became his friend. Later, Cézanne became a famous artist.

In 1858, Émile Zola moved to Paris to study at the Lycée Saint-Louis. His mother wanted him to become a lawyer. But Zola was not a good student. He failed his baccalauréat examination twice. Zola's first job was as a clerk[1]. He worked for a company that moved goods through France and sent them overseas.

Between 1860 and 1862, Zola wrote poetry and worked for the publishing company, Hachette. While he was working there he wrote a book about his own life called *La Confession de Claude*. After this he had to leave his job. The police read the book and said that it was unsuitable – it described unpleasant and private things. It was while Zola was working as a journalist that he met Gabrielle-Alexandrine Meley. Zola married her in 1870.

Émile Zola wrote non-fiction books and articles as well as fiction. He was interested in politics and people's lives. In some of his articles, he spoke against the government and its leaders. In his novels, Zola wrote about relationships. He believed that novels should tell the truth about families, and about love and sex. He described how people's lives can change when they meet and love the wrong person. The people in Zola's novels show strong feelings – love, jealousy[2], anger, hate and joy. His stories describe affairs[3] and murders, successes and failures. Zola wrote about working people, poor families with only a little education, and women who were paid to have sex. Many readers were shocked by these stories. When Zola wrote *L'Oeuvre* (The Masterpiece) – a book about artists and writers, his friend Cézanne became angry and their friendship ended. However, by the beginning of the twentieth century, Zola was recognized[4] as one of France's greatest writers.

Between 1871 and 1893 Zola wrote twenty novels about the history of two families. The stories were about the Rougons, who were tradespeople[5] and the Macquarts, who were smugglers[6]. Zola showed what happens when simple people become rich and successful and then they are destroyed[7] by their troubles. The Rougon-Macquart books were extremely successful and Zola earned a lot of money. He bought a house and land in Médan.

In 1888, Zola began an affair with Jeanne Rozerot and they had a family of two children.

During Zola's life, many changes were taking place in the world. While he was studying in the Lycée Saint-Louis, Emperor Napoleon the Third became leader of France. Then, in 1870, the country became a republic again. In the 1880s, writers, scientists, politicians and artists in France were all thinking about new ideas. And French art and painting changed in the middle of the nineteenth century. Painters started to use a softer and brighter style of painting. The style of painting was called Impressionism and the artists were called Impressionists. These artists wanted to show the things that happened in the lives of ordinary people. They painted pictures of the waiters, dancers, and the men and women who spent time in the bars, wine-shops and cafés of Paris. They showed families enjoying themselves in parks and by rivers at weekends.

In 1894, a Frenchman called Alfred Dreyfus was accused[8] of the crime of spying[9] for Germany – an enemy of France. Dreyfus was taken to a court of law. There was a trial and he was found guilty[10]. Dreyfus was sent to prison. Zola didn't believe that Dreyfus was a spy. In 1897, he wrote a letter to *Le Figaro* newspaper. He said that Dreyfus should have another trial. Later, Dreyfus did have another trial, and he was found not guilty. But in 1898, Zola himself went to prison for a year and he had to pay three thousand francs. He escaped[11] to England and lived in London for a year.

On 29th September 1902, Émile Zola died. He died because gas and smoke from the stove in his bedroom came into the room and the air became poisonous[12]. Some people thought that Zola's death was an accident. Other people believed that he had been murdered by an enemy of Alfred Dreyfus. Fifty thousand people came to Zola's funeral.

Thérèse Raquin was published in 1867 when Zola was twenty-seven years old. At the time that it was published, the novel shocked many people. It is a story about adultery[13], madness, ghosts and revenge[14]. Some of Zola's other books are: *L'Assommoir* – The Drunkard (1871); *Le Ventre de Paris* – The Belly of Paris (1873); *Le Roman Experimental* – An Experimental Novel (1880); *Nana* (1880); *Pour Le Bonheur des Dames* – For Women's Delight (1883); *Germinal* (1885); *La Terre* – Earth (1887); *Le Rêve* – The Dream (1888); *La Bête Humaine* – The Human Beast (1890); *L'Argent* – Money (1891); *Le Débâcle* – The Downfall (1892).

The People in This Story

Madame Raquin

Camille

Thérèse

Old Michaud

Olivier Michaud

Suzanne Michaud

Grivet

Laurent

François

1

Vernon

The Raquin family lived in the town of Vernon, in Normandy[15]. Madame Raquin had a small drapers shop[16] in the town, where she worked hard for nearly twenty-five years. Madame Raquin's business was successful and she was able to save money. Then her husband died and Madame Raquin became a widow. A few years later, she decided to sell her business and have an easier life.

After she had sold the business, Madame Raquin had quite a lot of money. With some of this money, she was able to rent[17] a little house with a garden. The house stood on a bank[18] of the River Seine. The pretty garden went down to the river and the house was surrounded by fields and trees.

Madame Raquin was now more than fifty years old and she lived happily in her quiet little house with her son, Camille, and her niece, Thérèse. Camille Raquin was twenty years old and Thérèse was a few years younger. Camille Raquin had been ill all his life. He was small and thin, with a pale, blotchy[19] face.

Camille's mother had spoilt[20] her son when he was a child. She had worried about him and she had done everything for him. He had had many illnesses and she had looked after him with great care. She still treated[21] him as if he was a sickly[22] child.

Camille had often been too ill to go to school and he had not been well educated. His empty mind was as weak[23] as his body. Camille's mother wanted her son to stay at home with her for ever. But he wanted to meet other people. When he was eighteen, Camille had got a job as a clerk in a small office. The boring work pleased the stupid young man.

Camille thought of nothing and no one but himself. His mother did everything for him, but he did not love her. He was now a selfish and vain[24] young man. Camille was a man, but his body was as weak as a child's. His pale face, with its thin red beard, always had a stupid, angry expression[25]. But Madame Raquin's feelings for her son had never changed. She had loved the sickly child. Now she loved the selfish, stupid, young man. This love made Camille angry with his mother and he was often rude to her. Madame Raquin did not care. Her love for her son was the most important thing in her life. She would always look after Camille.

Thérèse Raquin was Madame Raquin's niece. Thérèse's father had been a captain in the French army. He had spent many years fighting in North Africa. In Algeria, he had met and married Thérèse's mother, a beautiful Algerian woman.

Sixteen years ago, Madame Raquin had been surprised when her brother had come to her house in Vernon. He was holding a two-year-old child in his arms.

'Here is Thérèse, my little daughter,' Captain Degans had said to his sister. 'The poor child's mother is dead, so I've brought my Thérèse home to France, and to you. I must soon return to the army in Algeria. There is no one to look after my daughter there. You are Thérèse's aunt and I'm asking you to help me. I'm giving my Thérèse to you. Please will you look after her?'

Madame Raquin smiled. 'I've always wanted a daughter,' she said. 'Leave the dear little girl with me. I shall love her as I love my own child. She can take my married name – Raquin. Your Thérèse and my Camille will grow up together in a safe and happy home.'

Thérèse grew up strong and healthy, but her aunt treated the girl like her sickly cousin. Madame Raquin kept both children in warm rooms. Sometimes she made Thérèse take Camille's medicine.

'Thérèse,' Madame Raquin often said to her niece, 'Camille is ill again. Sit quietly by the fire so that Camille can sleep.'

Thérèse had grown into an unusual-looking young woman. She had thick black hair and large dark eyes. Her face was pale and she had a long nose and pale thin lips. Sometimes, eighteen-year-old Thérèse looked very plain. But at other times she looked very beautiful.

Every evening, Camille came home from his office to eat the meal that his mother had made for him. Then the young man sat looking at books until it was time to sleep.

Thérèse never read books and Camille thought that she was stupid. The two young people almost never spoke to each other.

Every evening, Thérèse would sit calmly and silently. The young woman wanted to run and dance, but she did not. Sometimes she sewed[26] some clothes. Sometimes she did nothing. Sometimes Thérèse just sat looking at the flames of the fire. François, Madame Raquin's big tabby[27] cat, sat and stared at the fire too.

Madame Raquin was pleased with her quiet, family life. She was happy and cheerful. Every evening, she did her sewing and made careful plans for the family's future.

'I'm so pleased that your father brought you to us,' Madame Raquin said to Thérèse one evening. 'And I'll be very happy when you and Camille marry. That is my dearest wish, Thérèse. And I know that you will be happy together. But we'll wait until you are twenty-one, my dear.'

Thérèse nodded[28], but she said nothing. She looked across the room at Camille, but he had fallen asleep.

———

On warm days in the summer, Thérèse sometimes went down to the river. She lay in the long grass on the river bank. She looked like a cat who is waiting to catch a mouse.

Sometimes Thérèse just sat looking at the flames of the fire.

Thérèse loved to feel the heat of the sun. She loved to watch the water of the river and listen to the sound that it made. Thérèse felt more alive. But she kept all these strong feelings to herself. No one ever knew her thoughts.

In the Raquins' little house by the fast-flowing river, every day was the same. Every day was quiet and peaceful.

Camille sometimes became angry with his mother. She was always worried about his health. Sometimes on summer evenings, Camille would take Thérèse walking by the river. He held her hand and pulled her along the path. He laughed at her and tried to make her angry. Sometimes he pushed her off the path.

One evening, Camille pushed his cousin so hard that she fell to the ground. Thérèse jumped up as quickly as a cat. Her eyes were bright with anger and she hit Camille hard with her fists[29]. The sickly young man fell to the ground and looked up at the girl in surprise. He was very frightened. He never tried to make Thérèse angry again.

———

Soon Thérèse was twenty-one and it was time for her to marry Camille. Madame Raquin spoke kindly to her young niece when they were alone.

'You don't remember your father or your mother, my dear,' Madame Raquin said. 'Your father was a brave[30] soldier and he fought and died for his country. I never knew the lady who became his wife. But she must have been beautiful, like you, Thérèse.

'Your father and mother only had a short time together,' Madame Raquin went on. 'I hope that you and my son will be married for many happy years!'

Thérèse stood up and kissed her aunt. But the strange, quiet girl did not say a word.

And so Camille and Thérèse were married. On the night of her wedding, Thérèse did not go to her own bedroom.

She walked quietly into her cousin's bedroom. That was the only way that her life changed.

The next morning, Camille walked downstairs as calmly as usual. He took no notice of[31] his wife. Thérèse behaved[32] as she had always done. She was silent and her face did not show her thoughts or feelings.

2

The Passage du Pont-Neuf

A week after his marriage, Camille told his mother about his plans for the future.

'Until now, you have planned my life for me,' Camille said rudely. 'I've taken all the medicines that you have given me and I've never complained[33]. I'm a married man now, but you still treat me like a child. I want things to be different. There's going to be a change in all our lives. I'm going to live in Paris. You and Thérèse are coming with me!'

Madame Raquin was very surprised. 'My dear Camille, I've lived in Vernon all my life!' she said. 'I've worked hard and made a good home for us here in the country[34]. I don't want to live in Paris.'

'But I do,' Camille replied. 'That is what I want. We will leave Vernon at the end of the month.'

No one asked Thérèse what she wanted.

Madame Raquin did not sleep well that night. But she thought carefully about her son's words. She wanted Camille to be happy. Then she would be happy too. Soon Madame Raquin had a plan of her own.

'This is what we will do,' she said cheerfully the next morning at breakfast. 'I'll go to Paris tomorrow. I'll look for a

13

small drapers shop that we can rent. Thérèse and I can work in the shop. It will keep us busy. You can work, if you want to, Camille, or you can just enjoy yourself in Paris.'

'I'll get a job,' Camille said. He wanted to be a clerk in a big, important office. He wanted to talk to other young men.

Madame Raquin went to Paris the next day. A friend had told her about a drapers shop in the centre of the city. The shop was in a little arcade[35] called the Passage du Pont-Neuf[36].

Paris was big and noisy. Madame Raquin was frightened by the busy streets, the big shops and the crowds of people. At last she found the Passage du Pont-Neuf.

The little arcade was narrow and dark. And the little drapers shop was dark too. But Madame Raquin felt safe there and the business was being sold very cheaply[37]. The shop's rent was not expensive and the rooms above the shop could be rented cheaply too. Madame Raquin decided that her little family could live very comfortably in the Passage du Pont-Neuf.

By the time that Madame Raquin got back to Vernon, she was feeling very cheerful and excited. She was happy to have her own business again and every night she talked about her plans.

'Oh, my dear Thérèse, we'll all be so happy living in that little arcade,' Madame Raquin said. 'It's a quiet place, but it's in the centre of Paris. There are three fine rooms and a kitchen above the shop. The shop itself will keep us both busy! We'll arrange our goods in the very best ways. And our name will be painted on the front of the shop in red letters: Raquin – Drapers.

'The arcade is always full of people,' Madame Raquin went on. 'We'll have lots of customers all day. We'll never be bored!'

As Madame Raquin talked to her niece, she forgot that the shop was small and dark. As usual, Thérèse said nothing.

14

She waited to see the place herself.

Not long after this conversation, the Raquins left their peaceful home in Vernon and went to live in Paris.

The Passage du Pont-Neuf was a dark, narrow arcade between two high black walls. The arcade was about two metres wide and thirty metres long. It was paved[38] with damp, cracked[39] stones and its glass roof was black with dirt. During the day, very little light came through the roof of the arcade. In the evening, the narrow passage was lit by three square lanterns[40]. The lanterns gave a strange yellow light. When the wind blew, the lanterns made shadows that moved along the walls.

Narrow shops were built along the left wall of the arcade. These little shops were dark and damp. The shop windows were made of squares of dirty green glass. It was almost impossible to see the goods – cheap clothes, old books, toys and paper – that were inside the shops. On the right wall of the arcade there were narrow cupboards. Many kinds of different goods lay on the dirty brown shelves of these cupboards.

No one walked slowly through the Passage du Pont-Neuf. No one went there to enjoy shopping. Servants and tradespeople hurried through the passage. They always wanted to get somewhere else quickly. Their shoes made a loud noise on the stone paving.

When Thérèse went into the drapers shop for the first time, she felt sick and ill. The dark, damp place felt like an open grave[41]. The girl stood and looked at everything in the narrow little shop. There was a counter[42] on one side and a spiral staircase[43] on the other. All round the walls, there were green boxes, and cupboards with glass doors.

Thérèse went slowly up the spiral staircase to the rooms above the shop. There was a sitting-room, two bedrooms and a very small kitchen. In the sitting-room, there was a stove and a table, with four chairs standing round it. Everything was old and dirty.

Thérèse walked into each room and then sat down in despair[44]. Her body was stiff[45] with shock and horror. She felt cold and dead inside. She wanted to cry, but she could not. This awful place – this narrow shop and these few small rooms – was her new home. She was going to live here for the rest of her life!

Madame Raquin knew that she had made a mistake. She knew that she should not have rented the shop. But she tried to speak cheerfully to Camille and Thérèse.

'The arcade looks dark because the sun isn't shining today,' she said. 'And the shop's dirty now, but we can soon clean it. Choose some new wallpaper[46] for the rooms upstairs, Thérèse. We can get new curtains and carpets too. We'll put flowers in every room, my dear!'

'Why should we do that?' Thérèse said sadly. 'We'll be comfortable as we are. We don't have to change anything.'

'The place is all right,' Camille said to his mother. 'We'll only be upstairs in the evenings. I'll be at my office all day. You and Thérèse will be busy in the shop all day. You won't be bored.'

———

Camille looked forward[47] to leaving the Passage du Pont-Neuf every morning. *He* was going to work in a warm and comfortable office every day. Every evening, he would come home, eat his dinner and go to bed early.

Madame Raquin arranged all the furniture in the rooms above the shop. Then she cleaned the shop. It was a month before Camille got a job. But while he was looking for work, he stayed away from the shop all day. He did not return home until the evening. At last he found a job as a clerk with the Orléans Railway Company. He was going to earn one hundred francs a month. The young man was delighted.

Camille left home at eight o'clock every morning. He enjoyed the long walk to his office, along the banks of the River Seine. He enjoyed his time away from the shop, his mother and Thérèse. Everything in Paris pleased the stupid young man. In the evenings, he walked very slowly back to the Passage du Pont-Neuf.

Madame Raquin and Thérèse sat behind the counter of the dark little shop, day after day. Madame Raquin often fell asleep and the tabby cat, François, slept on the counter beside her. Thérèse sat quietly, without moving. Her pale face became paler and paler. She never complained.

Cheap clothes, women's hats and stockings[48] were for sale in the little drapers shop. There were piles of green wool[49]. There were knitting-needles, boxes of buttons and cheap ribbons[50]. Madame Raquin tried to arrange all of the goods in an interesting way, but business was bad. There were not many customers and the shop did not make much money.

Thérèse smiled sadly when she served[51] the poor girls who were their customers. Madame Raquin talked to everyone cheerfully. The customers always wanted Madame Raquin to serve them.

Days passed and every day was the same. And for Thérèse Raquin, every morning was the start of another boring day in the Passage du Pont-Neuf. The cheap goods in the shop became damp and dirty. Thérèse saw the dark, sad days going on and on to the end of her life. Every evening, she sat silently upstairs in the sitting-room. At ten o'clock, Madame Raquin went downstairs to lock the door of the shop. When she came up the stairs again, she kissed her son and his wife, and went happily into her bedroom. François, the cat, went to sit on his chair in the kitchen. Then the family went to bed.

Thérèse followed Camille into their bedroom. Every evening, she walked across the room and opened the window.

*Thérèse saw the dark, sad days going on
and on to the end of her life.*

She stood there for a minute, looking out at the high, black wall. Then she closed the shutters[52] and turned towards her husband and their cold bed.

―――

One day in the week was different from the others. Every Thursday evening, the Raquins had visitors. Thursday evening was the most important time of the week. The Raquins and their visitors played dominoes[53], talked and drank tea. The visitors left late in the evening and the Raquins did not go to bed until eleven o'clock.

Their visitors were always the same people. The first was Old Michaud. He had known Madame Raquin in Vernon and he had been the Police Commissioner[54] there. He was now retired[55] and living in Paris. One wet day, soon after they had moved to Paris, Michaud had met Madame Raquin outside her shop. He was soon visiting the Raquin family every Thursday.

After a few weeks, Michaud brought his son Olivier, who worked in the police department, to the drapers shop. Olivier was a tall, thin young man, about thirty years old. Suzanne, Olivier's pale little wife, came with him.

Grivet was a friend of Camille. He worked for the Orléans Railway Company with Camille. Grivet was an important man in the railway's office and Camille respected[56] him. Camille hoped that, one day, he would get Grivet's job.

Every Thursday evening was the same. At seven o'clock, Madame Raquin went into the sitting-room and lit the fire in the stove. Then she put a big lamp in the middle of the table. Beside the lamp, Camille put the box of dominoes. Chairs were moved from along the walls and put round the table. Then Madame Raquin prepared the cups and saucers for tea.

At eight o'clock exactly, Old Michaud and Grivet met outside the little shop and went inside. Then everyone went up the spiral staircase to the sitting-room, sat down round the table, and waited for Olivier Michaud and his wife. They always arrived late.

When all the guests were in the sitting-room, Madame Raquin gave everyone some tea. Then Camille took the dominoes out of the box, put them on the table, and the game began.

The only sound came from the dominoes as they were moved about on the table. At the end of every game, the players talked about it for a few minutes. Then there was silence as the next game began.

Thursday evenings were terrible for Thérèse. She hated their visitors and she hated playing dominoes. Thérèse was so unhappy that she played the game badly. This made Camille angry with her.

Thérèse would often pick up François, the big tabby cat, and hold him in her arms. Sometimes Thérèse said that she had a headache[57] and could not play. Then she would sit, half-asleep[58], with her elbow on the table and her hand against her face.

Thérèse stared at the people round the table and their ugly faces made her half-mad. She could see them clearly in the yellow light of the lamp. Old Michaud's face was pale, with red blotches on it. He was a very old man, and in the light of the lamp, he looked half-dead. Grivet's stupid face was narrow and he had round eyes and thin lips. Olivier had a small head on his long, stiff body. Suzanne's face, with its small eyes and pale lips, was soft and white.

'None of these people seem alive,' thought Thérèse. 'They are like ghosts.'

Thérèse found it difficult to breathe in the quiet room and this terrified her. She sometimes had a feeling that they were all buried together, deep under the ground.

There was a little bell on the door of the shop. It rang

every time that a customer entered. Every Thursday evening,
Thérèse hoped that a customer would come into the shop.
She listened for the sound of the shop-bell. When she heard
it, she would run downstairs and stay in the shop for as long
as possible. The damp air of the shop cooled the heat of her
face and hands. She would sit down behind the counter in
her usual place, and forget everything.

Camille was angry when his wife left the sitting-room.
After a time, he would go to the top of the stairs and shout
down to Thérèse.

'What are you doing down there?' he would say. 'The
customer went a long time ago. Come up at once! Grivet has
just won another game and we need you up here!'

Then Thérèse would get up slowly and return to her place
at the table in the sitting-room. She would pick up the tabby
cat and hold him in her arms. At eleven o'clock, the four
visitors would leave the Passage du Pont-Neuf. Then
Madame Raquin would lock the door of the shop and walk
slowly back up the stairs.

3

A New Visitor

One Thursday evening, Camille returned from his office
with a tall young man who had a black beard and thick
black hair.

As usual, Madame Raquin and Thérèse were sitting in
the shop.

'Well, Mother,' Camille said. 'Do you recognize this fine
young man? You used to give him bread and butter when we
lived in Vernon!'

Madame Raquin looked at the man and shook her head.

'No, Camille. I don't know this gentleman,' she said.

Thérèse stared at the visitor too.

'Well, it's a long time since you saw him,' Camille said with a laugh. 'It was twenty years ago. This is little Laurent, the son of Old Laurent, the farmer. Laurent used to go to school with me in Vernon. He came to our house nearly every day!'

'I'm sorry that I didn't recognize you!' Madame Raquin said to the visitor and she smiled. 'I'm very pleased to see you, Laurent. Welcome to our home. I can't call you "little Laurent" now. You are too tall! Sit down and tell me where you met Camille.'

'I work at the Orléans Railway Station, here in Paris,' Laurent replied with a smile. He sat down and looked around him happily.

'We both work for the same company – the Orléans Railway Company – but I didn't see Laurent until today,' said Camille. 'The office is very big and many people work there.

'Laurent's father sent him away to a school to study law,' Camille went on. 'But Laurent didn't want to be a lawyer. So then he studied art and painted pictures instead. Now he's got a job at the railway company. Laurent is doing very well there. He earns one thousand five hundred francs a month!'

Camille turned to Laurent. 'You must have dinner with us,' he said.

'I'd be delighted to dine with you,' Laurent replied.

Madame Raquin went upstairs to cook the dinner and Laurent sat in the shop with Camille and Thérèse.

Thérèse stared at Laurent without speaking. Camille's friend was tall and very powerful. His body looked firm and strong. He did not look like her weak, pale husband. Thérèse looked down at Laurent's big hands, then up to his short, broad neck. She looked at the young man's round, healthy face. She looked at his red smiling lips and his thick black hair. Laurent was the first real man[59] that Thérèse had ever seen. Her body shook with excitement.

'You must remember Thérèse, my wife,' Camille said. 'She's my little cousin. She used to play with us in Vernon!'

'I recognized her immediately,' Laurent said, looking into Thérèse's eyes.

Thérèse felt that Laurent could see into her heart. She smiled, stood up quickly and went upstairs to help her aunt.

At dinner, Camille asked his friend about his life in Paris.

'Well, at the beginning, I told my father that I wanted to study law,' Laurent said with a smile. 'He paid me an allowance[60] of one hundred francs a month. But I soon stopped studying law and I began to paint instead. I had met a friend who was an artist. I had been to school with this artist, who now had a studio in Paris. I was much happier when I was painting. But then my father found out that I wasn't studying law. He refused[61] to give me any more money.'

Madame Raquin went into the kitchen to prepare tea. Camille and Thérèse stared at Laurent in surprise.

'So did you get work as an artist?' Camille asked.

Laurent laughed. 'No. I'm afraid that I didn't,' he said. 'But I enjoyed myself for a time. I stayed all day in my friend's studio. There were always lots of beautiful models[62] there. My favourite model was a woman with long red hair and a fine body.'

Camille's eyes and mouth were now wide open. 'Did the model take some of her clothes off?' he asked.

'Yes, she did,' Laurent said. He looked at Thérèse as he spoke. Her face had become extremely pale.

'But my life as an artist wasn't successful,' Laurent went on. 'I couldn't earn enough money by painting. So I got a job in the railway office as a clerk. It's easy work and I make enough money to buy food. I'm glad that I'm not a farmer, like my father! I haven't seen the old man for years.'

Laurent was lazy[63] and selfish. He liked to eat good food, do very little work and make love[64] to women. Then he was completely happy. He tried not to smile as he looked at the surprised faces of Camille and Thérèse.

Thérèse's eyes were like two black holes in her pale face. Her mouth was open and she sat completely still. She was listening to every word that Laurent said.

'I've got an idea!' Laurent said to Camille suddenly. 'I'll paint your portrait[65]. I'll come here for two hours every evening. The painting will be finished in a week.'

Camille was delighted. 'You can have dinner with us every evening, Laurent!' he said. 'I'll curl[66] my hair and wear my best coat for the portrait.'

It was now eight o'clock and the Thursday visitors soon arrived to play dominoes. Camille introduced Laurent to Grivet and the Michauds and then they all sat down round the table. Laurent was careful. He behaved well. He laughed and told stories. He was soon everyone's friend.

The shop-bell rang once, but Thérèse did not leave her chair. She sat with the others, playing and talking, until eleven o'clock.

Thérèse did not look at Laurent again, but she felt uncomfortable and afraid. Laurent took no notice of her.

———

From that day, Laurent visited the Raquins every evening. The Raquins' sitting-room was warm and he always dined with them.

The young man was delighted. It was good luck that he had met Camille again. Laurent lived in a very small attic at the top of an old house. The room was cold and he had very little money for food. He usually spent the evenings sitting in a cheap café, smoking a cigar and drinking one glass of coffee with brandy[67].

*Laurent laughed and told stories. He was
soon everyone's friend.*

Now Laurent had a new home and a comfortable place to sit every evening. He ate dinner with the Raquins and enjoyed their company until ten o'clock. Then he walked slowly home to his little attic.

———

One evening, Laurent brought his easel and paints[68] to the Passage du Pont-Neuf. He prepared his canvas[69] and started to work on his portrait of Camille. Laurent had decided to paint the picture in Camille and Thérèse's bedroom.

'Good strong light comes through the window there,' he said. 'The sitting-room is too dark.'

Laurent was a very bad artist. He could not draw well. It took him three days to draw Camille's head. Then, on the fourth day, Laurent began to put paint on the portrait. He put spots and short lines of paint all over the canvas. Laurent's painting was worse than his drawing. The paints that he put on the canvas soon all became a dirty green colour.

The Raquins had never seen an artist working before. They thought that Laurent was very clever. Camille was very pleased with the portrait and he did not know how bad it was.

Thérèse stayed close to Laurent all the time. Every evening, she went into the bedroom and watched the young man working. She sat very still and did not say a word. Laurent noticed all this and now he began to think about his future.

'Thérèse is a young woman who needs a lover,' Laurent said to himself on his way home one evening. 'Her husband doesn't please her. She's a passionate woman – she has very strong feelings. Her eyes show this. And she's bored in that shop. She likes me. One day, she'll find a lover. Perhaps that lover should be me. I'll kiss her and see what happens.'

Laurent walked on and then he thought again.

'Thérèse Raquin is not beautiful and I don't love her,' he

said to himself. 'But she might be an interesting lover. However, I must be careful. The Passage du Pont-Neuf is an awful place to live. But I enjoy going there in the evenings. The sitting-room is warm and comfortable and Madame Raquin is a good cook. I don't want to lose all that. I must think carefully before I do anything.'

Finally, Laurent made a decision – he would try to seduce[70] Thérèse.

'I'll wait until we're alone,' he said to himself, 'and then I'll kiss her. She won't tell her husband. But *if* Camille finds out, I can knock him down and leave!'

Several evenings passed, but Laurent could not kiss Thérèse. He was never alone with her.

At last the portrait was finished and Laurent and the Raquin family looked at it together. The picture was very bad, but the Raquins did not understand that. Laurent had made the painting of Camille's face look very strange. The face was covered in green and brown paint and the mouth was twisted[71]. It looked like the face of a drowned[72] man.

But stupid Camille was delighted. 'You've made me look very unusual,' the vain young man said to Laurent. 'Now I'm going to buy two bottles of champagne and we can all have a drink together!'

He ran downstairs and out of the shop. A few minutes later, the shop-bell rang and Madame Raquin went to serve a customer in the shop.

Thérèse stayed in the bedroom, looking at the portrait of Camille. Laurent was collecting his brushes and paints. Seconds passed. Suddenly, the young man turned round. Thérèse was standing very close behind him.

Thérèse and Laurent looked at each other for a few moments. Their faces were only inches apart. Then Laurent pulled Thérèse towards him. He put his hand in her hair and pulled her head back as he kissed her hard on the lips.

At first, she fought him. She tried to push him away and hit him. Then suddenly she stopped fighting him and fell to the floor. Neither of them said a word. Their love-making was silent and brutal[73]. And it changed their lives for ever.

4

Love

From the evening that the painting was finished, Laurent and Thérèse made love whenever they were alone. They felt as if they had been lovers for years. Thérèse made careful plans. She could not leave the house, so Laurent came to the Passage du Pont-Neuf.

'We can meet here, in my bedroom,' Thérèse said calmly. Then she pointed at a door across the corridor. 'Behind that door, there are some stone stairs. They lead down to a little alley[74] which goes into the arcade. I'll leave that door open for you.'

'When shall I come?' Laurent asked. He was surprised by Thérèse's behaviour. She was calm and careful. She knew exactly what to do.

'You must leave your office in the afternoon,' Thérèse said to her lover. 'Madame Raquin will be serving in the shop and Camille will be at work. Be careful when you go into the alley. No one must see you. Come tomorrow.'

The next day, Laurent told his manager at the railway office that he had to leave work for two hours. He walked to the Passage du Pont-Neuf and went towards the drapers shop. When no one was looking, Laurent walked quickly into the alley behind the shop. He ran up the stone stairs.

The door opened and the light of a lamp shone onto Thérèse, who was standing at the top of the stairs. She was

Thérèse was standing at the top of the stairs.

wearing only her white petticoats[75]. Her thick black hair was tied behind her head.

As Laurent stepped inside, she shut the door and put her arms around him. She smelt of violets[76].

Laurent was amazed. He had never seen Thérèse like this before. She was strong and beautiful. Her eyes shone with the madness of love and her body shone in the light.

From their first kiss, Thérèse had shown Laurent how passionate she was. No one had taught her how to be a lover, but she understood how to love a man.

Thérèse was a married woman, but her husband was weak and cold. Camille had no desire[77] for his wife. Now, with her strong and passionate lover, Thérèse's mind and body were awake for the first time.

Laurent had never known a woman like Thérèse. She almost frightened him. When Laurent left Thérèse that afternoon, he walked like a drunken[78] man.

Laurent decided that he would not visit Thérèse again. It was too dangerous. Then he thought of her holding out her arms to him and welcoming him to her bed. He knew that he could not keep away from her. From that day, Thérèse became part of Laurent's life.

———

Thérèse was completely happy and she had no fear. She told Laurent all her thoughts. She told him everything that had ever happened to her.

'I've been unhappy all my life,' Thérèse said one day. 'I was a strong and healthy child. But I was treated like that weak, sickly Camille. My aunt made me drink his medicine. I slept in the same room as him.

'Madame Raquin has been kind to me,' Thérèse went on. 'She looked after me, when my father could not. But I wanted fresh air, not hot rooms. I wanted to run and dance and shout. But I had to sit quietly all day, because of Camille. I liked the little house by the river at Vernon. I liked the river too. It was strong and powerful, like you.

'My mother was Algerian,' she continued. 'I'm sure that she was a passionate woman. I am passionate too. You know that now. But the Raquins turned me into a silent, stupid thing. Sometimes I was mad with anger. I often thought about throwing myself into the river. I thought about running away from Vernon. But I did nothing. The Raquins' kindness almost destroyed me. But then we came to this dark, damp hole. We came to this awful shop. My mind was dead.'

Thérèse was so excited, that she had begun to shout.

'Don't make so much noise!' Laurent whispered. 'Madame Raquin will hear you!'

Thérèse laughed, but she stopped talking for a moment and walked about the room. Then she went up to Laurent and held his strong hands in her two small hands.

'Why did I marry Camille?' she said. 'He has never been a real husband to me. He has never loved me like you do. I was afraid of you at first. I could not show my feelings. I waited for you to do something. But now I have you – and I love you! My heart is alive. My mind is alive. *I'm* alive! Madame Raquin can come up to this room. I don't care!'

Laurent was not very happy about his visits to the Passage du Pont-Neuf. But he returned every afternoon, week after week. He had to see Thérèse and make love to her. He could not stay away.

Then, one day Madame Raquin came up to the bedroom when Laurent was there.

Thérèse had been upstairs for three hours and her aunt was worried about her. Laurent heard the old lady coming up the spiral staircase. He jumped off the bed and started to pick up his clothes.

Thérèse laughed. She pushed him and his clothes onto the end of the bed.

Then she threw the bedclothes[79] and her petticoats on top of him.

'Stay there and don't move,' she said.

Thérèse got back onto the bed, just as the door opened. She covered her body with the bedclothes and pretended[80] to be asleep.

'Thérèse, my dear, are you ill?' Madame Raquin asked her niece kindly.

Thérèse opened her eyes slowly and turned her head towards her aunt.

'I have a terrible headache,' she said in a quiet voice. 'Please leave me. I want to sleep.'

Madame Raquin left the room without saying another word. The lovers laughed and kissed each other.

'You see, we've nothing to fear,' Thérèse said. 'No one can see what is happening between us. They cannot see how we love each other!'

On another afternoon, François the cat was with them. He sat in the middle of the bedroom and watched the lovers with his bright green eyes.

'Look at François,' Thérèse said. 'Do you think that he understands? Does he know that we are lovers? Perhaps he'll tell Camille everything this evening!'

'Cats can't speak,' Laurent said quickly. He did not like cats and he was a little afraid of François.

'How can you be sure?' Thérèse said with a laugh. 'Think of all the stories that François could tell about us! He watches us with his big green eyes. He has seen us make love many times.'

Laurent looked at the cat and felt afraid.

'Look, this is what François will do,' Thérèse said. She stood up and held up her hands. She made the noise of a cat.

'He'll stand on his back legs and point at us with his feet like this,' Thérèse said. 'Then he'll say, "Laurent and Thérèse were kissing each other in the bedroom this afternoon. They thought that I did not understand, but I did. Put them into prison at once!'"

Thérèse laughed again and moved her body like a cat. François stared at her with his green eyes and Laurent thought that the cat was smiling.

Laurent got up quickly, opened the door, and put the cat into the corridor. He was afraid of the animal and sometimes a little afraid of Thérèse too. He did not understand her.

———

Laurent thought that his life was perfect. Every afternoon, he made love with Thérèse in the bedroom above the drapers shop. Every evening, he left work with his good friend Camille, and walked back to the Passage du Pont-Neuf.

Madame Raquin always greeted Laurent cheerfully. She treated him as her own son and gave him a good dinner every day.

In the evenings, Laurent talked to Thérèse politely, but she never smiled at him when they all sat together.

Laurent was now the wife's lover, the husband's friend and the mother's spoilt child. He had everything that he wanted and he was part of the family too. He did not think about the future – he was enjoying himself too much.

Thérèse was nervous about her affair with Laurent. But she was used to hiding her feelings. She had been hiding her feelings for most of her life. She knew that she and Laurent were doing wrong. But she enjoyed deceiving[81] Camille and his mother. When Laurent was in the house, Thérèse's face became plain and cold. She spoke to her lover rudely. But when Laurent was not in the house, Thérèse could show her happiness. She sometimes sang and she often laughed.

Thérèse bought flowers and put them in her bedroom. She put new wallpaper on the walls. She asked her aunt for new carpets and new curtains. She wanted fine new furniture.

She did all these things to please Laurent.

'Camille and Laurent are good friends,' thought Madame Raquin. 'I feel as if I have two sons, not one.'

Thérèse's face was calm and still. But her mind was full of thoughts of her lover and their afternoons of love-making. The young woman laughed to herself. She was happy that she was deceiving her husband and her aunt.

When Camille and Madame Raquin went downstairs, Thérèse jumped up from her chair and kissed her lover on his lips. When she heard the Raquins coming back to the sitting-room, she sat down again. Her face became completely still and calm once again.

On Thursday evenings, Thérèse talked to the visitors and played dominoes cheerfully. Laurent behaved well too and the others all enjoyed his company.

As the visitors got ready to leave, Thérèse and Laurent whispered together. They made plans for their next meeting. Sometimes they were alone for a few seconds and she kissed him.

This life of passion and calm lasted for eight months. Thérèse was never bored. She no longer felt cold and dead inside. And Laurent was happy and well-fed.

5

Saint-Ouen

One afternoon, Laurent's manager spoke to the young man angrily.

'You've been spending too much time away from the office,' the manager said. 'We pay clerks to work, not to go out every afternoon. You must stay in the office all day. If you leave your desk again, you'll lose your job.'

Laurent was going to see Thérèse that afternoon, but he did not want to lose his job. He needed the money. He knew that his father would not give him an allowance now. Laurent did not move from his desk all day.

In the evening, he went quickly to the Passage du Pont-Neuf. Thérèse looked at him angrily, but he was not able to speak to her alone for some time. When Laurent *was* alone with Thérèse for a few minutes, he spoke to her quietly.

'We can't meet again!' Laurent whispered. 'My manager won't let me leave the office.'

Then Camille came back into the room and Laurent could not say anything more.

Thérèse did not sleep that night. She lay in the bed beside Camille and tried to think of a plan. On Thursday, she told Laurent when she wanted to see him, but he did not come.

___

Two weeks passed. Thérèse had only one thought in her mind – she wanted to be alone with Laurent again.

Laurent was like a wild animal in a cage. He was half-mad because he could not hold Thérèse. Laurent loved her and he could not live without her. He had never felt like this before. His desire for Thérèse was very strong. He needed her in the same way that he needed food and drink. He could not go to the Passage du Pont-Neuf in the evenings now. He was frightened that he would show his feelings. He thought that Camille and his mother would find out about his affair with Thérèse.

Then Thérèse wrote to Laurent. She told him to stay at home the next evening. She would come to his room at eight o'clock.

The next afternoon, Laurent spoke to Camille as they were leaving the office of the Orléans Railway Company.

'I'm sorry, my friend,' he said. 'But I'm very tired. I think that I'll go home. I will not dine with you tonight.'

Thérèse told Madame Raquin that she had to go out.

'A lady bought several things this morning but she didn't pay for all of them,' Thérèse said. 'I know where the customer lives, so I'm going to her house. I'll get the money. I'll be out for about two hours, I think.'

Madame Raquin did not like losing money. 'Very well, my dear,' she said to Thérèse. 'But be careful. You don't go out in the evenings very often.'

Thérèse put on her coat, hat and gloves and went towards the house where Laurent lived. She walked quickly, pushing people out of her way. Thérèse's face and hands were very hot and she walked like a drunken woman.

Thérèse ran up the stairs of the house where Laurent lived. When she reached the sixth floor, she was breathing very fast. Laurent was standing there, waiting for her. Thérèse ran into the attic and her wide skirts almost filled the little room. She took off her hat and fell onto the bed.

The little attic had a skylight[82] in the roof. The cold evening air came in through the window and cooled the room and the two lovers. They stayed together until the bell of a church clock rang ten times. Thérèse wished that she had not heard it. She got up slowly, found her hat and put it on. Then she sat down on the bed again. Laurent knelt on the floor in front of her.

'I must go,' Thérèse said. 'Goodbye.' But she did not move.

'Don't just say goodbye. Tell me when you are coming back,' said Laurent.

Thérèse looked into her lover's eyes. 'I don't think that I can come back,' she said.

'So we must say goodbye for ever?' Laurent asked quietly.

'I don't want to say goodbye,' Thérèse replied. Then she repeated, 'I must go.'

Laurent thought about Camille, but he did not want to say his name.

'I don't dislike him, but he is a problem,' Laurent said. 'Why can't he go away? Can't you send him on a journey?'

'A journey?' Thérèse said sadly. 'Camille will never leave the Passage du Pont-Neuf. He will never leave home until he goes on his last journey – the journey that no one comes back from. You know what I mean. But he'll live longer than all of us. Sickly people always live the longest.'

'I want to spend the whole night with you,' said Laurent. 'I want to sleep with you every night. I want to be with you forever. I want to be your husband.'

Thérèse kissed Laurent and then she began to cry.

'Help me to be strong!' Thérèse cried. 'Say that you love me and that one day we'll be together. Please tell me that you need me!'

'I do need you. Come back tomorrow,' Laurent said.

'That is not possible,' Thérèse replied. 'But perhaps I'll tell Camille everything and then I'll leave him. I'll come back here and live with you. I don't care what people say about me. I want you to be happy.'

Laurent began to think more clearly. Thérèse could not live with him in his little attic. It was too small. And if she left the Passage du Pont-Neuf, he could never visit the Raquins again.

Laurent spoke slowly. 'If your husband was dead, we could be happy together.'

'If ... if he was dead,' Thérèse repeated. She looked down at her lover. Her eyes looked very dark in her pale face.

'Sometimes, people die suddenly,' she said. 'But there might be a problem for the family later.'

'I'm not stupid,' Laurent said quickly. 'I want to live with you and love you in peace. Perhaps your husband could have an accident. People have accidents every day. But we must be careful. I'll think of a plan.'

They both stood up and Thérèse walked to the door. Laurent put his arms around her.

'You are mine, aren't you?' he said. 'You belong to me?'

'Yes, I belong to you. Do what you like with me,' Thérèse replied.

They stood there silently for a moment. Their love for each other was wild and dangerous. Then Thérèse pulled herself away from Laurent's arms and ran down the stairs.

Laurent lay down on the bed again. The bedclothes were warm and smelt of violets. He lay on his back and looked up through the skylight at the square of dark blue sky. He did not sleep that night. Before Thérèse's visit, he had not thought of killing Camille. Now, because of his desire for Thérèse, he could only think of killing her husband. He thought about what could go wrong. He thought about what would happen to Thérèse and himself. He thought about his father.

'Perhaps my father will live for another ten years,' Laurent said to himself. 'And when he dies, I might not get his money. I can't go on living in this room, working in the office, and living on cheap food for ever. But if Camille was dead, I could marry Thérèse. Madame Raquin would call me her son and I'd get her money. And I might get my father's money too, when he is dead.'

Laurent wanted Thérèse. He did not want to share[83] Thérèse with her husband, Camille. If Camille disappeared, Laurent could become Thérèse's husband. Camille must be killed. But no one must know who had killed him.

'I must kill him. I must kill him,' Laurent said to himself again and again, until he fell asleep.

Thérèse got home at eleven o'clock. She could not remember getting back to the Passage du Pont-Neuf. She felt cold and very ill. Madame Raquin and Camille were worried about her, but Thérèse would not answer any of their questions.

Thérèse's body shook with cold and fear when she got into bed with Camille. He fell asleep at once and lay there with his mouth open. Thérèse hated him. Camille was her husband and she wished that he was dead.

———

Three weeks passed. Once again, Laurent started visiting the shop every evening. Madame Raquin welcomed him as usual, but she said that he looked tired. Thérèse did not speak to Laurent. She made herself look as ugly and stupid as Camille. Madame Raquin was worried by the girl's silence.

'Take no notice of Thérèse's cold behaviour,' the old woman said to Laurent one day. 'Sometimes, she is not friendly, but she has a warm heart.'

The lovers did not make plans to meet each other. Their faces were calm, but their hearts were full of anger and fear. They could not speak to each other about their true feelings – feelings of murder and desire.

Sometimes, when they were alone, Laurent and Thérèse held each other's hands for a moment. They held hands so tightly, that they hurt each other. But they did nothing more. They were waiting.

One Thursday evening, Old Michaud, the retired police commissioner, began to talk about unsolved crimes[84].

'I could tell you about some terrible crimes – including murder – that are still unsolved,' the old man said.

'Do you mean that there are killers walking in the streets?' Grivet cried. 'Are there murderers who have never been caught?'

'They have not been caught, because no one knows that they *are* murderers,' Olivier said. 'We try to find them, but the police can't catch everyone. There are some murderers who will never be caught. Their crimes will never be solved. These murderers are too clever.'

Laurent and Thérèse listened to this conversation, but they did not say anything. They looked at each other and Thérèse shook with fear.

———

Sometimes, on Sundays, when the weather was fine, Camille made Thérèse walk with him along the wide streets of Paris. The stupid young man liked people to look at his beautiful wife. But Thérèse hated going out with her husband.

Madame Raquin was always worried when Thérèse and Camille left the Passage du Pont-Neuf. She would follow them slowly to the end of the arcade and then call out, 'Be careful! There is a lot of traffic[85] in Paris these days. So many people have accidents. Look where you are going!'

Then the old woman would walk very slowly back to the shop and she would worry until Camille and Thérèse returned.

Laurent began to go with Thérèse and Camille on these Sunday walks. Sometimes, the three of them left Paris and found a café on the banks of the Seine. They would have a meal and walk by the water.

Thérèse loved to walk by the River Seine. She loved to sit on the grass and put her hand in the water. She loved to breathe the warm, sweet air.

One Sunday in the autumn, Camille, Thérèse and

Laurent left the arcade at eleven o'clock. On this day, the sky was blue and the sun was warm. Laurent, Camille and Thérèse were going on a longer visit. They rode in a cab[86] across Paris and then they walked to Saint-Ouen. When they reached this small town to the north of Paris, Camille and Thérèse walked along the warm, dusty road beside the River Seine. Camille had one hand on his wife's arm. In his other hand, he held a parasol[87] over Thérèse's head. Laurent walked behind them. Sometimes he looked down at the road. Sometimes he looked at his lover.

The three young people walked along one bank of the river. Then they went over a little bridge to a small island and looked for a comfortable place to sit down. They found a quiet place, where grass was growing under tall trees. Red leaves had fallen from the trees. The leaves made a dry, crunching noise as the young people walked over them. The island was quiet and peaceful. The cool green water of the river flowed round and past the island.

Camille sat down on the soft grass. Thérèse dropped down onto the ground and her wide skirts spread round her in a big circle. Laurent lay on his stomach and looked at Thérèse. He could just see one of her legs beneath her wide skirts. Her leg was slim and beautiful, with its white stocking and black shoe.

The three of them – Laurent, Camille and Thérèse – stayed on the island for three hours. They waited for the cool of the evening.

At first Camille told the others silly stories, but at last, he fell asleep. He lay on the ground, with his hat over his eyes and his mouth wide open.

Laurent moved closer to Thérèse. He kissed her shoe and then her leg. Thérèse smelt of violets and desire burned through Laurent's body like fire. He wanted to hold his lover in his arms, but he could not. Camille might wake up.

41

Thérèse smelt of violets and desire burned through Laurent's body like fire.

Laurent thought that Thérèse was asleep. He stood up, went over to a tree and leant against it. Then he saw that Thérèse was not asleep, her black eyes were wide open. Laurent stared down at her, but she did not look at him.

Laurent looked at Camille. The silly, weak young man looked ugly and stupid and Laurent hated him. He lifted his foot above Camille's face and Thérèse gave a cry. Laurent put his foot back on the ground. It would be stupid to murder Camille like that. Laurent walked down to the fast-flowing river and stared at the water. Then suddenly, he had a plan.

'I can murder Camille and never be caught,' Laurent thought. 'Then I'll be able to enjoy the rest of my life with Thérèse. My plan is perfect!'

Laurent woke his sleeping friend and told him to stand up. Thérèse stood up too and shook the red leaves from her dress.

'Let's go and get something to eat. I'm hungry,' Laurent said.

They left the island and walked along little roads that were full of happy, laughing people. The sun was not so bright now and the air was getting cooler. Camille and Laurent walked together and Thérèse walked more slowly behind them. She was sure that Laurent had a plan and she felt very frightened. Thérèse's legs shook and she felt weak.

'Come on!' Camille shouted to Thérèse. 'I'm hungry. Aren't you?'

'Yes,' Thérèse replied, but she was not hungry. She was too frightened.

They soon found a cheap little café on the river bank. The lower floor of the café was full of customers, so they went upstairs to a terrace[88].

6

The Accident

Thérèse, Laurent and Camille sat on the terrace and looked down at the many people below them. Waiters were running about, serving customers with food and wine. Girls wearing brightly-coloured dresses were dancing and shouting. There were some students who were watching the girls and laughing at them.

The sun was setting now and the sky was as red as fire. Far away, the hills above the city were blue.

Laurent started to call for a waiter, but then he stopped.

'Why don't we go for a boat-trip[89] on the river?' Laurent said suddenly to Camille. 'Then we can come back and eat here later.'

'Thérèse is hungry now,' Camille said.

'I can wait,' his wife replied quietly.

The three friends walked down the steps of the terrace and spoke to a waiter. They ordered their meal and told him that they would return in an hour.

The owner of the café hired out[90] boats. Laurent chose a very narrow rowing-boat[91] and the café-owner untied the rope that held it to the river bank.

Camille and Thérèse looked at the boat.

'Is this boat big enough for all of us?' Camille said. 'We'll have to sit very still, or one of us will fall in!'

'Are you frightened?' Laurent asked, laughing.

'No, of course not,' Camille replied.

But Camille could not swim and he was afraid of water. He got into the little boat very carefully and sat at the far end of it. Laurent turned towards Thérèse. As she stood on the bank beside the boat, he whispered to her.

'Don't be afraid. I'm going to push him into the river.

Don't worry. I'll do everything.'

Thérèse's face became very pale. She could not move.

'Thérèse is frightened,' Camille said with a laugh. 'Look at her, Laurent! Will she get in the boat or not?'

Camille's words made Thérèse angry. She jumped into the boat and sat at the opposite end to Camille. Laurent sat down in the middle of the boat and picked up the oars. As he pulled the oars, the boat moved away from the bank and towards some small islands. Soon the boat was in the middle of the River Seine.

The sun was very low now and the sky was getting dark. The black shadows of the trees fell across the water. It was colder too. Laurent stopped rowing and the fast-flowing river moved the boat along. Laurent, Camille and Thérèse sat in silence as the sky and the river became darker.

Camille was lying on his back. He put his hand into the fast-flowing water of the Seine. 'That's cold!' he said. 'I wouldn't like to fall in there!'

Laurent did not answer. He was sitting completely still, with his big hands on his knees. Thérèse sat at the other end of the boat. Her body was stiff with fear.

Now their boat was moving into a narrow space between two of the small islands. There were no other boats here. Laurent stood up and moved to the end of the boat where Camille was sitting. He put his hands on Camille's waist.

'What are you doing?' the young man said, laughing. 'Be careful, Laurent! I shall fall into the water!'

Then Camille saw the cold, cruel expression on Laurent's face and he was terrified. Laurent put one hand around the weak young man's throat. Camille shouted out.

'Help me! Thérèse!'

Thérèse sat very still. She held onto the sides of the boat with both of her hands. She wanted to shut her eyes, but she could not. The little boat moved from side to side.

'Help me! Thérèse!'

'Thérèse!' Camille cried out again.

Thérèse could not watch what was happening. She felt shocked and ill. She fell down into the bottom of the boat and began to cry.

Camille held the sides of the boat tightly, but Laurent pulled his hands away. Then he picked up Camille and held the weak young man like a child. As Laurent bent his head forward, Camille bit him on his neck. With a cry of pain, Laurent threw Camille into the water. Camille screamed two or three times, as his head came up out of the water. Then there was silence.

Laurent moved quickly. He took hold of Thérèse and pushed the narrow rowing-boat over. As the boat rolled over, Laurent and Thérèse fell into the cold water.

'Help! Help!' Laurent shouted loudly.

Laurent was strong and a good swimmer. He was in no danger. He easily held Thérèse in his arms as he swam to the the river bank. Some men in another boat heard his cries and they rowed towards Laurent and Thérèse as fast as they could.

Laurent and Thérèse were soon safely on the bank. Thérèse had fainted[92] but Laurent jumped into the water again. He began to look for Camille. He looked under the rowing-boat and around it. But he was careful to look in the wrong places. Laurent came back to the river bank alone.

'It was my fault[93]!' Laurent cried. 'My friend Camille moved in the boat too much. Then he stood up! I should have stopped him. He didn't understand the danger. The boat turned over. As Camille fell into the water, he called out to me. "Help my Thérèse!" he shouted.'

'Yes, we saw it all!' some of the young men said.

This was not true. The young men had not seen anything, but they wanted to feel important. They helped Laurent to turn his rowing-boat over again so that it lay safely in the water once more.

47

'The poor woman has fainted,' said one of the young men, looking at Thérèse. 'Someone must look after her.'

The young men tied the narrow rowing-boat to their own boat and pulled Laurent and Thérèse back to the café. Very soon, everyone in Saint-Ouen knew about the accident. They knew that Laurent's friend – Thérèse's husband – had fallen into the river and disappeared.

The young men described the accident exactly as Laurent had told them the story. Everyone thought that the young men had seen the accident and so everyone believed Laurent's story. The owner of the café and his wife were kind people. They gave Laurent some dry clothes. Thérèse could not stop crying and shaking and they put her into a bed.

Laurent left Thérèse in Saint-Ouen and went back to Paris alone. He wanted to tell Madame Raquin the terrible news himself. He did not want Thérèse to tell Camille's mother. He wanted Thérèse to become calm and think more clearly.

'Thérèse will say too much,' he thought. 'She might make a mistake and tell Madame Raquin the truth.'

Laurent went back into Paris on an omnibus[94]. As he rode back into the city, he thought of the story that he was going to tell Madame Raquin. He was a little worried, but he was happy too. Laurent was sure that people would believe his story. It had been a perfect murder. No one would ever know the truth.

———

Laurent got off the omnibus when it reached Paris. Then he took a cab to Old Michaud's house. Laurent had decided that he did not want to tell Madame Raquin about Camille's death himself. It would be safer to have Michaud with him.

It was now nine o'clock in the evening and Michaud was having dinner with Olivier and Suzanne. Laurent told them his terrible story. He pretended to be shocked and unhappy.

He wept as he walked up and down the Michauds' dining-room.

'I've come to you for help,' Laurent said with tears in his eyes. 'You are the Raquins' closest friends. Those two poor women! Thérèse is suffering[95] already. Madame Raquin will suffer too, when she hears the terrible news of her son's death. I don't know what Madame Raquin will do. Please come with me, so that we can tell her together.'

Olivier stared at Laurent but he said nothing. Laurent suddenly felt a little afraid of the police official. But Olivier believed Laurent's story.

'Oh, poor Camille!' Old Michaud cried. 'What a terrible accident! How will Madame Raquin live without her son? She loved Camille so much!

'You came to us,' the old man went on. 'That was the right thing to do. We are Madame's friends. We'll go with you at once.'

They went together to the Passage du Pont-Neuf. When they arrived at the arcade, Old Michaud stopped Laurent.

'Wait here,' the old man said. 'If Madame Raquin sees you without Camille and Thérèse, she'll know that something terrible has happened. Wait here for us.'

Laurent waited for half an hour. He walked up and down the damp, narrow street outside the drapers shop. Suddenly, he felt very hungry. He went into a bakers shop, bought some cakes and ate them quickly.

In the little drapers shop, Madame Raquin listened to Old Michaud tell the story of her son's death. She screamed and wept. The mother thought only of her poor son who had drowned in the fast-moving water of the River Seine. She had saved his life so many times when he had been a child. And now he had died without her. He had drowned in cold dirty water. As she thought about it, Madame Raquin wanted to die too.

Old Michaud and Olivier left Suzanne with the old woman and went to find Laurent. Then the three men took a cab back to Saint-Ouen. The journey was terrible for all of them and no one spoke.

———

In the café by the river bank, Thérèse could not get out of bed. Her body was shaking and her skin was burning hot. She had a fever. Thérèse was terrified that she might confess[96] to the murder. So she had made herself ill. Her mouth and eyes were tightly shut and her body was curled in the bed like a baby.

In her mind, Thérèse could see her lover, Laurent. She could see him murdering her husband, Camille. It was like a terrible dream. She saw the murder happening again and again. She thought that she could see Camille rising up out of the dirty water and coming towards her.

Old Michaud tried to talk to Thérèse, but she turned her face away and began to weep again.

'Let her sleep, sir,' the café owner said. 'She needs to rest.'

In the café, a police officer was asking questions about the accident. When Olivier told the officer that he was an important police official, no one asked any more questions.

Several people said that they had seen the accident happen. But they were only repeating Laurent's lies. Everyone believed Laurent's story. He was not going to be accused of any crime. He had nothing to fear now, and he knew this.

'We can't leave poor Thérèse here,' Laurent said to the Michauds. 'We must take her back to Paris with us.'

Laurent went upstairs to talk to Thérèse. He repeated her name several times. When Thérèse heard her lover's voice, she gave a cry and opened her eyes. She looked terribly ill, but she sat up and looked at Laurent.

The café-owner's wife helped Thérèse to get dressed.

Then Thérèse walked slowly downstairs and Olivier helped her into the cab.

On the way home, no one spoke. It was dark inside the cab and Laurent held Thérèse's hand tightly. Thérèse was very frightened and she sat very still. But she did not take her hand away. When the cab stopped, Laurent whispered to Thérèse.

'Be strong, Thérèse,' he said. 'Remember. We have a long time to wait.'

'Oh, I'll remember,' she replied quietly.

Laurent went with her to the shop and left her there with Olivier. Madame Raquin was in her bedroom where Suzanne had been looking after her. Suzanne came down the stairs and took Thérèse up to her own bedroom. The young widow fell onto her bed and lay still.

It was now after midnight. Laurent walked back through the empty streets to the house where he lived. Everything had gone well and he felt pleased with himself. Camille was dead and no one thought that he had been murdered.

'Everything is perfect,' Laurent said to himself. 'I've killed Camille but no one knows that I'm his murderer. Now I must wait for a few months and live alone. Then I can marry Thérèse and we can begin our new life together.'

Laurent felt very tired as he walked up the stairs. When he reached his little attic room, he lay down on his bed and fell asleep at once. The murderer slept well that night.

7

The Morgue

The next day, Laurent woke up feeling very cheerful. Only one thing was troubling him. The place on his neck where Camille's teeth had broken the skin was sore. The bite-mark was red and it was very painful. Laurent washed off the blood and turned up the collar of his shirt to hide the mark. Then he put on his suit and necktie and went to his office as usual. He told everyone in the railway office about Camille's death and how it had happened. The story was reported in all the Paris newspapers. Laurent was a hero.

———

Laurent was only worried about one thing. Camille's body had not been found and so a death certificate[97] could not be signed. If the body of a dead person was found, it was taken to the Paris Morgue. The corpse was kept in this cold, damp building for several days. People went to the morgue to see if the dead body of a friend or relation had been found in a street or the River Seine. The morgue was a horrible place, but Laurent now went there every day. He was sure that Camille's body would soon be found in the river.

The dead bodies lay on huge blocks of stone, with cold water running over them. There was a wall of glass between the corpses and the people who came to look at them.

Every day, Laurent moved slowly along the glass wall. He looked carefully at all the bodies of the people who had been found in the river, but he could not see Camille.

Laurent began to have bad dreams because of his visits to the morgue. He went there every day for more than a week, and every night he had dreams. Then, on the tenth day, he saw Camille's body there. It was lying on one of the cold, wet blocks of stone.

Camille's body was lying on one of the cold, wet blocks of stone.

When he saw Camille's body, a terrible pain went through Laurent's heart. The drowned man's eyes were open and he seemed to be looking at his murderer.

For more than five minutes, Laurent stared at his dead friend. Camille had been in the water for some time and his corpse was a horrible sight. His face was still smooth, but his skin was brown and green. Camille's body had many terrible green and black wounds on it. His head was twisted to one side and his black lips seemed to be smiling.

Laurent turned away and left the morgue quickly. He felt sick.

'I made Camille like this,' Laurent said to himself. 'I've never seen a more horrible sight. I thank God that I won't have to see his corpse again!'

Laurent went to Old Michaud, and told the retired Police Commissioner what he had seen. No one thought that Camille had been murdered. They did not believe that a crime had been committed. They believed that Camille had died in a terrible accident. So the officials at the Paris Morgue wrote and signed a death certificate and Camille's body was buried.

Laurent thought that he could stop worrying. Now he could forget about the murder! He decided to enjoy himself. He began to look forward to the future.

———

After the death of Camille, the drapers shop in the Passage du Pont-Neuf was closed for three days. Madame Raquin and Thérèse stayed in their beds for two days. They did not speak and they did not see each other. Suzanne Michaud looked after the two women. But she could do very little to help them.

Camille's death had been terrible for Madame Raquin. For twenty-four years, she had looked after her sickly son. Because of her care, Camille had not died when he was a child. Then, in a few minutes, the young man had been taken away from his mother. Sometimes the old woman sat up in her bed and stared at the walls of her room. She did not speak and her face looked like a pale corpse. At other times, she screamed and wept. Sometimes she called out Camille's name as she slept.

Thérèse lay in her bed, stiff and silent. Her face was always turned towards the wall and she pulled the bedclothes over her eyes. She did not speak and she did not weep. On the third day, Thérèse suddenly sat up in her bed. After a few seconds, she threw off the bedclothes and got out of the bed.

At first her legs were weak and she could not stand. Then she slowly walked towards a mirror[98] which was on the wall and looked at her face. Her pale skin was blotchy and she looked much older.

Thérèse pulled her hair away from her face and tied it behind her head. Then she dressed quickly and went to Madame Raquin's bedroom. The old woman turned her head and looked at her niece. Then she held out her arms to Thérèse and kissed her.

'My poor child! My poor Camille!' she said.

Madame Raquin began to weep loudly. Thérèse knelt on the floor and hid her face in her aunt's bedclothes. She stayed completely still for a few minutes. Thérèse had been very afraid of her first meeting with the old woman, but all seemed to be going well. She stood up and spoke to Madame Raquin for the first time.

'My dear aunt, you must try to get up,' Thérèse said in a quiet voice. 'Everyone is very worried about you. You'll feel better if you go into the shop again.' At this moment, Suzanne Michaud came into the bedroom.

'Suzanne and I are here to help you,' said Thérèse. 'You have your other friends too. Let me get you something to eat now.'

Madame Raquin stared at Thérèse and then she began weeping again. When she spoke, the old woman sounded like a child.

'Thank you, thank you,' she said to Suzanne. 'Thank you for looking after me. And you, my dear Thérèse! You're unhappy too. I've lost my son, but you've lost your husband! We must always stay together now. We must always help each other.'

That evening, Madame Raquin got out of bed. Her legs felt very weak. She had to use a stick to help her to walk.

The next day, she told Thérèse to open the shop.

'I'll go mad if I stay in bed another day,' Madame Raquin said in a weak voice. 'We'll sit together in the shop again, my dear Thérèse. We must try to live.'

When the shop opened again, it seemed darker and damper than before. The windows were dirty and all the goods looked dirty too.

Every morning, Madame Raquin walked slowly down the spiral staircase. Then Thérèse helped the old woman to her seat behind the counter. Madame Raquin and Thérèse sat there all day. They did not move. People walked past the shop and saw Thérèse's calm, pale face as she sat at the counter. Everyone felt sorry for the young widow and her old aunt, Madame Raquin.

———

Every two or three days, Laurent visited the drapers shop in the Passage du Pont-Neuf. He came in the evenings and sat in the shop with Madame Raquin for half an hour. The old lady welcomed him. Laurent had been brave at the river. He had tried to help her son and he had saved her niece. During his visits, Laurent did not look at Thérèse or speak to her.

Laurent was in the shop at eight o'clock one Thursday evening when the Thursday visitors arrived. They had not met together since Camille's death.

Madame Raquin was surprised to see her friends, but she lit the lamp in the sitting-room and began to make tea. Everyone sat round the table. But when Grivet took the dominoes out of their box, the old lady began to cry.

'My dear lady, you mustn't cry,' Old Michaud said. 'You'll become ill and you'll upset your friends too.'

But Madame Raquin shook her head and went on weeping. Old Michaud spoke again.

'Madame,' he said. 'We've come here to help you. We want to help you to forget this terrible time. Let's play a game of dominoes!'

Madame Raquin decided that the old man was right. She continued crying, but she began to play dominoes with her friends.

Laurent and Thérèse watched and listened but they said nothing. Laurent wanted everything to continue as it had before Camille's death. He wanted to meet the same friends at the shop. He wanted to play dominoes with them on Thursday evenings. It made him feel safe. When other people were in the room, he was able to look at Thérèse again.

Thérèse was dressed in black clothes. The young widow looked very beautiful. Sometimes she looked calmly into Laurent's eyes. Laurent was happy. Thérèse still belonged to him.

———

Fifteen months passed. As the days went by, Laurent and Thérèse began to feel safe. Soon, Laurent was coming to the shop every evening after he finished work. But some things had changed. Laurent now arrived at about half past nine – after dinner. He stayed until Madame Raquin locked the shop. On Thursday evenings, Laurent went to the sitting-room before Madame Raquin's other guests arrived and he lit the fire in the stove. He looked after the old woman and did little things to help her.

Thérèse watched Laurent carefully. The young woman was more cheerful now. But sometimes her pale face had an expression of pain and terror.

Madame Raquin was not thinking clearly. The lovers could have done what they liked and she would not have known. But the lovers never tried to be alone together and they never kissed. The murder of Camille had killed their desire for each other. They no longer wanted to make love. When they were together, they did not know what to do or say.

Thérèse and Laurent tried to understand their feelings but they could not talk about them. The lovers thought that they were being careful and that their desire for each other would return. And now that Camille was dead, Laurent and Thérèse could get married. They believed that when they were married, they would have peace.

At night, alone in her bed, Thérèse was happy. Weak, stupid Camille was no longer there to make her angry. Thérèse felt like a little girl again. She felt safe in the big bedroom. Sometimes she opened the window and stared at the high black wall and the narrow strip of sky above it. Sometimes she had bad dreams. Only at these times did she think of Laurent. Thérèse did not desire her lover. She only wanted Laurent in her bed to keep her safe. She wanted Laurent because she did not want to be lonely. And she did not want anyone to think that she had killed Camille.

During the day, Thérèse was much happier. She became interested in the people around her and she talked more.

One day, Thérèse noticed a young man who lived near the Passage du Pont-Neuf. He was completely different from Laurent in every way. The young man was tall and slim, with fair hair and blue eyes. For a week, Thérèse was in love with this young man. But she never spoke to him and when he went away, she forgot about him.

Thérèse began to read books. She read romances and she fell in love with the heroes of these love stories. She began to think about other people and how they felt. But Thérèse could not understand her own feelings. She became nervous and worried about everything.

Laurent's feelings changed too.

'Did I really kill a man?' he said to himself. 'What a fool I was! I must have been drunk or mad. I committed a terrible crime. I did it for a woman and now I don't care about her at all!

'Well, I was clever, and I was lucky too. No one thought that I killed Camille Raquin. But I will never do anything like that again.'

Laurent became fat and lazy and he had no desire to make love with Thérèse. He wanted to get married because it would make his life more comfortable. When he came to live in the Passage du Pont-Neuf, he would have a bigger home, more money and good meals every day.

Then one day, Laurent met his old friend who was an artist and he began to spend a lot of time in the artist's studio.

When Laurent went to the studio, he saw that his friend was painting a picture of a pretty young woman. Laurent liked the artist's model, so he took her home with him. The girl became his lover and stayed with him.

Laurent did not love the model, but that did not worry him. He enjoyed making love with her and that pleased him. He never told Thérèse about the girl.

Then things changed again.

———

Thérèse no longer wore black clothes. She began to wear pretty, brightly-coloured dresses again.

One evening, Laurent noticed that Thérèse was looking younger and more beautiful. He also noticed that she laughed a lot and seemed very nervous. Sometimes she was very happy and sometimes she was very sad. Laurent did not like to see Thérèse behave in this way. He did not trust[99] her and he began to feel afraid.

Laurent began to think about marriage again. Sometimes he thought that he would not marry Thérèse. He thought that he would stay away from her and live with the pretty young model.

'But if I don't marry Thérèse,' Laurent thought, 'then I killed her husband for nothing! I'm a fool if I don't marry Thérèse now. She might go to the police and tell them everything. I can't let her do that.'

Then the model left Laurent. She moved out of his room and once again, Laurent was alone at night. After a week, Laurent went back to the drapers shop in the Passage du Pont-Neuf. He spent more time there and his desire for Thérèse returned. She looked at him with desire too. All their feelings for each other were strong again.

One evening, Laurent spoke to Thérèse as he was leaving the shop.

'I want you,' he said. 'I want to make love to you. Shall I come to your room tonight?'

Thérèse looked terrified. 'No, let's wait,' she said. 'We must be careful.'

'I've waited long enough,' Laurent replied. 'I want you,' he said again.

Thérèse stared at him. Her dark eyes shone brightly in her pale face. Then her cheeks became red.

'As soon as we are married, I'll be yours for ever,' she replied.

8

The Return of Camille

Laurent felt very worried as he left the little shop in the arcade. His desire for Thérèse had returned, but he was also very afraid of returning to his attic room. And for the first time, he was afraid of being alone. He went into a wine-shop and drank several glasses of wine. He was angry with Thérèse.

'I wouldn't be afraid if I'd stayed with her,' he thought. He turned towards a waiter. 'Bring me another glass of wine!' he shouted.

Laurent stayed in the wine-shop for many hours. Then he bought some matches[100] and walked home to his attic.

He had left a candle on a table on the first floor of the building. He had to go along a dark corridor, and up the stairs to the first floor to find his candle. He was terrified of the dark corridor. He believed that someone was waiting to kill him there.

Laurent struck a match and the flame gave a weak yellow light. Suddenly, the corridor became full of dark shadows. Laurent walked quickly up the stairs to the first floor and found his candle. He lit it and walked slowly up to the sixth floor, holding the candle in front of him.

When he reached his attic room, Laurent shut the door behind him. Then he closed the skylight and looked under the bed. The shadows in the room looked like people who were waiting to kill him. At last, he lay on the bed and began to think about Thérèse. He had to make a decision. Should he marry Thérèse, or not? He wanted to sleep, but his thoughts and fears kept him awake.

As he thought about Thérèse, Laurent's desire for her returned. He dreamt that he went back to the drapers shop in the Passage du Pont-Neuf. In his dream, he ran along the dark streets and into the arcade. He went through the alley and up the stairs to Thérèse's bedroom. Thérèse opened the bedroom door and stood there, waiting for him.

Laurent could see everything so clearly in his dream, that he sat up in his bed and cried out. 'I must go!' he shouted. 'Thérèse is waiting for me!'

He jumped out of his bed. The floor under his feet was very cold. Suddenly, Laurent felt afraid again. He was too frightened to leave his little room in the middle of the night. So he got back into the bed and pulled the bedclothes over his head. This quick movement made the bite-mark on his neck burn with pain. He touched the sore place and it reminded him of Camille. Laurent began to shake with fear. Perhaps Camille was in the room now! Perhaps he was under the bed!

Laurent sat up and lit the candle. Long, dark shadows moved on the walls.

'What a fool I am,' he said to himself. 'I shouldn't have stayed so long in the wine-shop. I drank too much wine. That's why I have been dreaming. I'll drink some water and try to sleep again.'

So Laurent drank some water, blew out the candle-flame, and lay down on the bed again. He felt calm now and he was sure that he would sleep. His body felt heavy and tired, but his mind was still busy.

Once more, he dreamt that he was on his way to the arcade in the Passage du Pont-Neuf. He ran along the little alley beside the shop and up the stairs. He knocked on the door and it opened immediately. But, oh, horror! It was Camille who opened the door! The corpse of his dead friend stood in the bedroom. Its skin was green and brown and covered in terrible wounds. Camille's body looked the same as when Laurent had seen it in the morgue!

The dead Camille held out his arms to his murderer and a laugh came from his twisted mouth. Laurent could see the dead man's black tongue behind his white teeth. Laurent woke up with a loud cry of fear. His bedclothes were damp from the cold sweat which covered his body.

'I must sleep,' Laurent said to himself. 'It will be morning soon.'

But every time that Laurent fell asleep, he had the same terrible dream. Again and again, the young man woke up and found cold sweat covering his skin.

At last he decided to get out of bed and get dressed. It was sunrise. Light was coming through the square skylight above the bed.

'I can't sleep because of Thérèse,' he said to himself. 'If she had let me stay with her, I wouldn't have had this terrible dream.'

After he had washed his face and got dressed, Laurent felt a little better.

'I'm not a coward,' he thought. 'I was strong and brave when I killed Camille. I wasn't afraid of him when he was alive. I'm not afraid of him now that he's dead. When Thérèse and I are married, I'll hold her in my arms and forget all about Camille.'

Laurent stood in front of a mirror and looked at the bite-mark on his neck. Camille's teeth had made the mark more than a year ago. But the sore place was still red and it felt very painful. Laurent turned up his shirt collar to hide the mark.

'I'll ask Thérèse to kiss my neck,' he said. 'Then the mark will disappear.'

Laurent felt very tired in the office all that day. He fell asleep many times.

'Poor Thérèse is very tired,' Madame Raquin told Laurent that evening. 'She did not sleep well last night. She had bad

Laurent stood in front of a mirror and looked at the bite-mark on his neck.

dreams and cried out while she was sleeping. When the poor girl woke up this morning, she felt ill.'

While Madame Raquin was talking, Thérèse came into the sitting-room. She looked at Laurent and he looked at her.

The ghost of Camille had visited Thérèse too. Her desire for Laurent had returned. But in her dreams, she had seen the terrible corpse of her husband.

Laurent and Thérèse had drowned Camille. His dead body would hold the lovers together for ever. They would never be able to escape from his ghost. They had to marry as soon as possible. Only then would the ghost of Camille leave them in peace.

———

The months passed. The lovers made a plan. They would not talk about marriage themselves. Laurent would continue to come to the Raquins' shop each evening. He would be kind and polite to Thérèse and her aunt. He would help them as much as possible. Soon Madame Raquin would believe that Thérèse should marry her husband's friend, Laurent. If the old woman suggested the marriage, there would be no problem.

As soon as Laurent and Thérèse were married, the ghost of Camille would leave them alone. That is what they believed. But they did not want to marry immediately. If they did, their friends might think about the relationship between Laurent and Thérèse. And then their friends might ask questions about Camille's death.

Every night, the lovers slept in their own beds. Every night, Camille's ghost came and they were unable to sleep.

Thérèse kept a lighted candle in her room. But the pale yellow flame did not stop the shadow of Camille's corpse from visiting her.

Laurent was afraid to go home and he sometimes walked through the streets all night. Whenever he slept, he dreamt that he was holding Thérèse in his arms. But then his dream changed and he saw that he was holding Camille's corpse.

Laurent and Thérèse became more terrified every day. But their desire for each other was like a burning fever.

Thérèse wanted to marry Laurent because she was afraid. And she needed Laurent and his kisses. Laurent wanted to marry Thérèse because he wanted an easy, comfortable life. He wanted to eat, drink, sleep and make love to Thérèse whenever he wished.

He also wanted money. He had not seen his father for years. He would never get any money from him. But Madame Raquin had about forty thousand francs. If he married her niece, Laurent would not have to work. For all these reasons, he had murdered Camille.

After several months, the lovers' plan began to work. Thérèse behaved like a sad, young widow. She moved slowly and she took no interest in anything. She said very little and she often wept.

'Perhaps Thérèse is ill. Perhaps she's dying!' Madame Raquin thought. She became very worried. The old woman had no other relatives. Madame Raquin feared that she would be alone if Thérèse died.

One Thursday evening, Madame Raquin told Old Michaud her fears.

'My dear friend, don't you know why Thérèse is behaving like this?' he said, laughing. 'Your niece is unhappy because she has been alone every night for nearly two years. She needs a husband!'

Madame Raquin could not believe these words. Did Thérèse want another husband now that her dear Camille had died?

'Make her marry as soon as possible,' Old Michaud said. 'Please believe me. I know that I'm right.'

Michaud's words made Madame Raquin cry. She cried for

her dead son and she cried for herself. She could not believe that people were forgetting Camille already.

But Thérèse's unhappiness was making the old woman unhappy. Madame Raquin liked people to be cheerful and friendly. She wanted her niece to be happy again. But she did not want a stranger in her family.

Laurent came to the shop nearly every day. He helped Madame Raquin as much as possible. Then he would sit for many hours and talk to her in a soft, kind voice.

Laurent also told the old woman that he was worried about Thérèse.

'Dear Thérèse is very ill,' he said sadly. 'I'm afraid that we will lose her soon. What will happen to us then? Poor Thérèse loved Camille very much. We all loved him! Your niece has been slowly dying for the past two years. Thérèse is getting weaker every day.'

Laurent almost believed his own words. Madame Raquin began to cry. At last, the poor mother began to think of Laurent as her son and she soon loved him as her own child.

———

On the next Thursday evening, Old Michaud noticed Laurent talking kindly to Thérèse. Michaud whispered to his old friend.

'Look, my dear Madame,' he said. 'Here is the husband that your niece should marry. Laurent should be Thérèse's husband. You must tell them this. We'll help you!'

Thérèse marry Laurent? Madame Raquin had never thought of this. But she understood immediately. It was a good idea! The three of them would be a perfect family.

All through the evening, Madame Raquin smiled at Laurent and her niece. The murderers knew that their plan was working well.

When they left the drapers shop that night, Old Michaud spoke to Laurent. He told him his idea about the marriage.

Laurent pretended to be very surprised.

'But Thérèse is the widow of my dear friend, Camille. Thérèse is like a sister to me,' Laurent said in a quiet voice. 'I couldn't marry her.'

'But you would take the place of your dear friend,' Michaud said. 'Thérèse needs a husband. And you are the only man that Madame Raquin likes and trusts. She will accept you. The marriage would please her very much.

'Thérèse was a good wife to Camille,' Michaud went on. 'She will be a good wife to you. You must marry her. We all think that this should happen.'

Laurent pretended to think for a moment.

'You're much older than me and I trust you,' he said. 'If the marriage will make Madame Raquin happy, then yes, I agree to it. I'll marry Thérèse Raquin.'

At the same time, Madame Raquin was talking to her niece.

'I've been a widow for many years,' the old woman said. 'I know that it's terrible to lose a husband, Thérèse. I loved my husband, and you loved Camille. I know that. His death was terrible and we will never forget it. But you are unhappy, my dear. Don't you ever think of marrying again?'

'Camille was my husband. No one can ever take his place,' Thérèse said quietly.

'I think that you're wrong, my dear,' Madame Raquin said. She was crying now and so was Thérèse.

'Laurent is already part of this family,' the old woman went on. 'He has been kind to both of us. We could all be happy together.'

'I want to please you, dear aunt,' Thérèse said. 'I love Laurent as a brother. But I'll try to accept him as a husband, if that will make you happy.'

She kissed Madame Raquin and held the old woman in her arms. The two women wept together.

The next morning, Michaud spoke to Madame Raquin outside the shop. They agreed that Thérèse and Laurent should get married.

Old Michaud was in the shop when Laurent arrived at five o'clock.

'Thérèse has agreed,' he whispered to Laurent. 'She will marry you.'

Thérèse looked up and stared at Laurent and he looked at her. Then Old Michaud went over to Madame Raquin and put his hand on her shoulder.

'Dear Madame,' he said. 'These two young people want to make you happy.'

Madame Raquin could not speak for several minutes. She held Thérèse's hand and placed it in Laurent's hand.

'I want you to get married,' she said. 'I want you, my dear niece, Thérèse, to marry dear Laurent. Then Laurent can be my true son.'

The guilty lovers' bodies shook as their hands touched.

'Thérèse, would you like to make your aunt happy?' Laurent asked.

'Yes,' Thérèse replied.

Laurent turned to Madame Raquin. 'When Camille fell into the water, he cried, "Help my Thérèse!"' Laurent said. 'He wanted me to look after her. I'm sure of that, Madame. I will marry Thérèse. I think that is the right thing to do.'

Thérèse could not listen to these words and she turned away. But Madame Raquin was weeping with happiness.

'Yes, yes. Make Thérèse happy, my dear,' she said to Laurent. 'My son thanks you from his grave!'

'Kiss each other,' Old Michaud said to Laurent and Thérèse.

Laurent kissed Thérèse and her pale face became red. This was the first time that anyone had seen them kissing each other.

By the following Thursday, all their friends knew about the marriage between Laurent and Thérèse.

'The marriage was my idea,' Old Michaud said. 'Laurent and Thérèse will be happy when they are husband and wife!'

Suzanne Michaud kissed Thérèse, and Grivet made a few stupid jokes. Laurent and Thérèse were polite to each other, but they did not show their true feelings. They carefully hid their desire.

Laurent wrote to his father. He hoped that Old Laurent would be pleased and that he would send his best wishes. But the old man said that he did not care about his son. He also said that Laurent would never get his money. When Madame Raquin heard this, she did a very stupid thing. She gave all her money – forty thousand francs – to her niece. She knew that Thérèse and Laurent would always look after her. The preparations for the wedding started at once.

9

The Wedding Night

The day of the wedding had come at last. Laurent and Thérèse woke up in their own rooms. They were both very happy. Their last night of fear was over.

It was December and very cold. Laurent was pleased that he was leaving his small, cold attic for ever.

'I will be warmer tonight,' he said to himself, smiling.

Madame Raquin had given him five hundred francs and he had spent most of the money on new clothes. Now, the young man washed and dressed carefully. As he was putting on his shirt, he felt a sharp pain in his neck. The old bite-mark made by Camille's teeth looked red and sore. Every time that he moved, Laurent felt a sharp pain.

When he was ready, Laurent got into a cab and went to the town hall[101]. At the town hall, the official asked Laurent and Thérèse if they wanted to marry each other. After Thérèse and Laurent had both agreed, the official spoke the rest of the words of the marriage ceremony[102], and the two young people signed a paper. Laurent and Thérèse were calm and quiet. They felt as if they were in a dream. They were married! They could forget about the past.

At six o'clock, Laurent, Thérèse and Madame Raquin met their friends in a café outside Paris. The new husband and wife could not believe what was happening. That night, they would sleep together in the same bed, and everyone would be happy. Thérèse and Laurent believed that their future would be comfortable and happy. They were too tired to think clearly. Madame Raquin was very happy. And she also believed that she would have a safe and comfortable future.

By half past nine, everyone returned to the little drapers shop. Thérèse went into her bedroom with Suzanne and Madame Raquin. Laurent stayed in the sitting-room with the men. He listened to Grivet's jokes and said nothing.

At last, Suzanne and Madame Raquin came out of the bedroom.

'Your wife is waiting for you,' the old woman said to Laurent.

Laurent stood up and shook his friends' hands. Then he walked into the bedroom like a drunken man.

———

Laurent shut the bedroom door behind him and looked across the room at Thérèse.

A bright fire was burning in the fireplace and a lighted lamp stood on a little table. All the bedclothes on the bed were smooth and white. There were big vases full of roses and the sweet smell of the red flowers filled the bedroom. The

71

room was a place for love – a place of calm and peace.

Thérèse was sitting on a small chair on the right of the fireplace and she was staring at the flames. She did not look at Laurent when he came into the room. Her white petticoats looked very bright in the light from the fire.

Laurent took off his coat and waistcoat. He walked towards Thérèse and kissed her on the shoulder. As his lips touched her skin, Thérèse's body shook. She turned and looked at Laurent with fear and disgust[103].

Laurent sat in a chair on the left side of the fireplace. Both lovers sat completely still for five minutes.

It was almost two years since Thérèse and Laurent had first been alone in this room. They had not made love since Thérèse's visit to Laurent's little attic. They had waited until this night – their wedding night. Now they could hold each other and kiss each other. But they did not. Their desire had turned to horror and disgust. They had killed a man and waited a long time for this moment. There was nothing to stop them loving each other, except their own feelings.

'Thérèse,' Laurent said, very quietly, 'do you remember those afternoons when we were in this room? I wanted to stay with you and fall asleep in your arms. And tonight that dream is coming true.'

Thérèse looked up at Laurent. This man was her husband now. But did she know him? In the fire-light, Laurent's face looked red. It looked as if it was covered with blood. Thérèse turned away.

'All our plans have succeeded, Thérèse,' Laurent went on. 'This is the beginning of our life together. Camille has gone for ever.'

Laurent made a terrible mistake when he said Camille's name. Immediately, the lovers felt that the ghost of the drowned man had come into the room. They felt that the corpse was sitting between them.

The bedroom was warm and smelled sweetly. But there was also the cold damp smell of death. They could not forget what they had done.

Thérèse looked at her new husband with fear and hate. Laurent realized that he had made a mistake and he began to talk about other things – the roses, the fire, anything that he could see. Thérèse tried to answer him. They were both afraid of their thoughts. They were both afraid of silence.

They could think of nothing and no one but Camille. Whatever they said aloud, the guilty lovers could not stop thinking about his death. Finally, they stopped talking. But the voices in their heads would not be silent.

'We killed Camille and his corpse is here between us. It will never go away.'

'Did – did you see him in the morgue?' Thérèse asked quietly.

'Yes,' Laurent replied.

'Was his body badly injured?' Thérèse asked.

Laurent remembered the terrible body of the drowned man, but he did not answer. He stood up and walked towards the bed. Then he walked back and held out his arms to Thérèse.

'Kiss me!' he said.

Thérèse stood up too. She leant against the wall. She tried to move her head away as Laurent came towards her.

'Kiss me. Kiss me,' he repeated.

Then Thérèse saw the mark on Laurent's neck. 'What's that?' she asked.

'It's – it's where Camille bit me,' Laurent said quickly. 'Kiss me, Thérèse. Kiss me there! Take away the pain.'

'Oh, no, no!' Thérèse cried. 'Not there. There's blood on it!'

She fell back down onto her chair. Laurent bent down and held her head in his big hands. He made her press her

They could think of nothing and no one but Camille.

lips against the mark on his neck. Thérèse did not move until Laurent let her go. Then she wiped her hand across her mouth and spat[104] into the fire.

Laurent turned away. He walked around the room for almost an hour. Thérèse sat in the chair without moving. They both knew the truth. When they had killed Camille, they had killed their desire for each other too.

The flames of the fire were weaker now and the room had become darker. As Laurent turned, he thought that he saw something in the corner of the room. Camille was there! He was standing in the dark shadow between the fireplace and a cupboard! His face was green and twisted.

'Look there!' Laurent cried, pointing at the shadows in the corner of the room. 'Look! It's Camille!'

'It's his portrait – the picture that you painted of him,' Thérèse replied very quietly. 'My aunt forgot to take it to her room.'

'His portrait?' Laurent repeated.

The portrait looked exactly like the face of Camille's corpse in the morgue.

'Take it off the wall! Take it away!' Laurent whispered.

'No, I can't,' Thérèse replied. 'I can't touch it. You must do it.'

But neither of them were able to touch the picture. They were too frightened.

Laurent started walking around the room again. Again and again, he looked at the portrait of Camille. Laurent was going mad with terror and despair.

Then Laurent heard a scratching noise[105]. He thought that the sound was coming from the portrait and he turned round quickly. Then he realized where the sound was coming from. Something was scratching at the door which led to the stairs. The drowned man was trying to get into the room!

The sound became louder and then there was a cry – the

cry of a cat! Madame Raquin's cat, François, had been asleep in the bedroom all this time. Now he was awake and he wanted to get out. Laurent moved towards the cat and François jumped onto a chair. The cat lifted his back and stood there. He looked at Laurent with his big green eyes.

Laurent did not like cats and he hated François.

'Don't hurt him! Thérèse cried.

A terrible idea had come into Laurent's mind.

'The ghost of Camille has entered the cat,' he thought. 'I must kill François.'

Laurent remembered how, more than a year ago, Thérèse had made noises like the cat. Did François really know the truth about them?

Laurent wanted to throw the cat out of the window. But he was too afraid to touch the angry animal with the bright green eyes.

The cat watched Laurent move across the room. Laurent opened the door and the cat ran out, crying loudly.

Thérèse watched as Laurent walked between the bed and the window. They did not want to get into the bed together. They did not want to touch each other. And that is how they spent the first night of their marriage.

Daylight came, bright and cold. Laurent felt calmer now. He took the portrait of Camille off the wall and turned it round. Laurent no longer felt afraid of the picture.

Thérèse went to the bed and pulled back the bedclothes. Her aunt must not know the truth. She must not know that they had not slept in the bed.

'I hope that we are going to get some sleep tonight,' Laurent said angrily. 'We've been behaving like frightened children. That can't happen again. It's all your fault. Try to be more cheerful tonight, do you understand?'

'I'll try,' Thérèse said quietly.

Laurent laughed, but he did not know why.

10

The Ghost

Laurent and Thérèse's wedding night was bad, but the nights that followed it were worse. They now both knew the truth. They would never escape from Camille. Their fear turned to anger, and everything that they said or did made the anger worse.

Before their marriage, Thérèse had been nervous and excited. Laurent had been calm and cheerful. He had eaten, drunk and slept like an animal. Nothing had worried him. Now he had become as nervous and frightened as Thérèse. He could not sleep. Terrible pictures of Camille were always in Laurent's mind. He was not sorry that he had killed his friend. But he was afraid of what was happening to himself.

In the daytime, he promised to be strong. But at night, when he was locked in the house with Thérèse, Camille was there too. Laurent saw frightening shadows in the corners of every room. His thoughts were making his body weak. His desire for Thérèse and his fears were making him mad.

Thérèse felt half-mad too. When she was a child, she had hidden her thoughts and feelings. After meeting Laurent, she showed the feelings that were in her heart. Now she felt guilty about Camille's death. She wanted to tell everyone what had happened on the river.

Laurent became afraid that Thérèse would tell Madame Raquin everything. His fear made him angry with Thérèse. When they were alone, he began to shout at her and beat her. He hit her again and again.

The guilty lovers could not lie in the bed. They sat by the fire or walked around the room. Sometimes they slept in the chairs. But they were terrified of lying together in the bed. In the mornings, their bodies were stiff and cold. Their faces were pale and blotchy. They both thought that they could see the terrible corpse of Camille. The drowned man was always between them.

A week passed in this way. Laurent and Thérèse fell asleep during the day and they were awake all night. The guilty lovers both pretended that this life and their behaviour was normal. But they were mad.

One evening, they were so tired that they lay down on the bed. The next night, they got under the bedclothes, but they did not touch each other. Thérèse lay down on one side of the bed, near the wall. Then Laurent lay down on the other side of the bed. There was a wide space between them. This space was for Camille. They believed that his corpse lay between them. They could feel the damp body. They were terrified of touching it.

Sometimes Laurent thought of holding Thérèse in his arms but the drowned man stopped him. Laurent thought that Camille was jealous of him.

One night, Laurent tried to kiss Thérèse. But she turned away from him and her body shook with fear.

'Why are you shaking?' he shouted. 'Are you afraid of Camille? Yes, you are, aren't you? You're afraid that he will come and pull you out of this bed! I'll take you to his grave one night. You can see his corpse for yourself. Then you will know that he can't harm you. Come! Kiss me! That will make you forget him!'

They kissed, but Thérèse's lips were as cold as ice. Laurent started to shake with cold too. Laurent could not kill Camille for a second time. Camille was a ghost. Laurent realized that Thérèse was not a widow. She was still married – married to a drowned man. Camille had destroyed them. They would never make love again. As they moved apart, they began to cry.

———

After Laurent and Thérèse were married, the domino games continued on Thursday evenings. The Michauds and Grivet came to the shop in the arcade as usual. Old Michaud and Grivet had been afraid that the domino games would end after Camille's death. They were delighted when they all met at the drapers shop as before.

Thérèse hated the visitors, but Laurent told her to be polite to them. Old Michaud had been a Police Commissioner in Paris and Olivier still worked for the police. The Michauds were important friends.

Laurent and Thérèse's days and nights had now changed completely. At night, they were terrified. But when day came, they pretended that they were happily married.

Every morning, Laurent got up and dressed quickly. After he had eaten his breakfast, he was ready for the day.

'Goodbye. I'll see you this evening,' he said cheerfully to Thérèse and Madame Raquin. And he went to his office at the Orléans Railway Company.

Spring had come and Laurent walked by the river. He enjoyed looking at the trees and the water. He enjoyed breathing the cool, clean air. He stayed in his office all day, but he did very little work.

In the evenings, as he walked back to the shop, his fears returned. Terror was waiting for him in the arcade.

After Laurent left every morning, Thérèse felt cheerful too. She cleaned the house and the shop and kept busy all day. Then Thérèse would cook lunch for Madame Raquin and herself.

In the afternoons, Thérèse would sit down behind the counter. The terrors of the night seemed very far away. She looked out of the shop window, into the arcade. Then she dreamt that she was buried in a cold grave with many other people. But she was alive and they were dead. This strange idea did not frighten her. She felt calm and safe. Sometimes

Suzanne Michaud came to see Thérèse. Later, Thérèse would cook Laurent's dinner. Then the fears of the night would return.

The evenings were very quiet. Laurent and Thérèse stayed in the sitting-room until it was very late. They did not speak to each other, but they listened to Madame Raquin telling them stories of her life in Vernon. She told Thérèse and Laurent her plans for their future too.

Madame Raquin sat in the light of the lamp. The young people sat in the shadows, looking at the old woman. But they never looked at each other. The sound of the old woman's voice almost stopped their fears.

On Thursday evenings, Laurent and Thérèse did not think about the terrors of the night because their friends were in the house. Thérèse would sometimes talk and laugh and Laurent would tell jokes.

But soon the guilty lovers had something different to worry about. Madame Raquin had been ill for some time. She could not move about easily and sometimes she could not speak clearly.

Laurent and Thérèse were worried. They were not sorry for the poor old woman, but they were sorry for themselves. The terrors of the night now began at six o'clock, when Laurent came home.

They looked after the old woman well. Everyone told Laurent and Thérèse that they were good and kind to Madame Raquin. But she became weaker every day.

―――

After four months, Laurent made a decision. He wanted to change his life. He had married Thérèse and stayed with her because he wanted the Raquins' money. But now he had an idea to make his life more enjoyable.

'I've something to tell you,' he said to the two women one evening. 'I've told my manager that I'm leaving the office. I don't want to work as a clerk any more. I'm going to start painting again. I've always wanted to be an artist.'

Thérèse looked unhappy. She knew that Laurent wanted money and she did not want to give it to him.

'How much money will you earn?' Thérèse asked. 'The shop doesn't make much money, you know.'

Laurent looked at his wife. She understood him at once.

'Well,' she began, 'I might be able to give you a little money each month ... '

'Of course, Laurent must have some money,' Madame Raquin said kindly. 'He could be a great artist. He needs your help, Thérèse.'

'I'll have to rent a studio,' Laurent said quickly. 'Just a small one at first. Then I must buy new paints and brushes. One hundred francs a month would be enough.'

Laurent rented a studio the next day. Two weeks later, he left his job at the Orléans Railway Company.

The studio was small, but Laurent could be alone there. He did not start painting immediately. He did nothing. One day, Thérèse visited him in the studio, but he pretended to be out. In the evening, he told her that he had spent the day at the Louvre museum.

After a few weeks, Laurent bought paints and canvases and started to work. He could not pay for a model, so he drew and painted pictures from his imagination[106].

Laurent usually painted in the mornings. In the afternoons, he walked around Paris. On one of these walks he met an old friend. The man was a successful artist and he was making a lot of money.

'Why, it's you, Laurent!' the painter cried in a surprised voice. 'I didn't recognize you. You've become thin and pale.'

'I got married,' Laurent said. 'And I've started painting again.'

'Well, your marriage must be very successful,' the artist

said, with a laugh. 'You look very well and you are better dressed too! Let me see what you are painting.'

'Come to my studio now,' Laurent said. 'I'm starting a big picture.'

The artist was very surprised by Laurent's work. 'These drawings of faces are very good,' he said to Laurent. 'Your work is much better now.'

The artist looked at the painting again.

'There is something strange about the faces,' he said. 'The faces are of men and women, but they all look the same. Change some of them. Then they will be good.'

When his friend had left, Laurent looked at the painting carefully. His face became pale and he suddenly felt very cold.

The faces *were* all the same – they all looked like Camille!

Laurent picked up a new canvas and drew another face. Again, it was Camille's face who looked back at him.

With a cry of terror, Laurent picked up a knife. He began to cut the pictures into many pieces. He could never be an artist. He would never paint again.

Laurent looked down at his hand. Whatever he tried to do, every painting would look like Camille. Camille would always be with him in his studio.

With a cry of terror, Laurent picked up a knife.

11

Madame Raquin

Madame Raquin had been ill for some time. Then she had a stroke[107]. She stopped speaking in the middle of a sentence and she never said another word again. She also became paralysed – she could not move any part of her body, except her eyes.

Laurent and Thérèse were shocked and upset. But they were sorry for themselves, not for the poor old woman. From that day, their lives became worse. Madame Raquin's happy conversation had given them peace. Now she was silent and they lived with the ghost of death all the time.

The light of the lamp fell on Madame Raquin's round pale face. Thérèse and Laurent sat in the shadows and watched the old woman. When Madame Raquin shut her eyes, they woke her up. The old woman's eyes seemed to be the only living things in the room.

Thérèse looked after her aunt carefully and gently. She fed her and dressed her. She tried to understand what the old woman needed. Every morning, Laurent carried the silent old woman into the sitting-room and she sat there all day. Then Laurent went to his studio and Thérèse sat in the shop. In the evenings, they all sat together in the sitting-room.

The Thursday evenings went on as usual. Madame Raquin's friends talked to her. They pretended that nothing had happened. They pretended that she was talking with them.

Madame Raquin could not move and she could not speak. But she was happy because her children were looking after her. Her eyes were bright with joy. The only person who understood the old woman was Thérèse. She watched her aunt's eyes carefully and tried to help her.

Madame Raquin lived like this for several weeks. She thought that nothing worse could happen to her. But she was wrong. Laurent and Thérèse became careless. They began to talk about Camille so that the old woman could hear their conversation.

'Is he there in the shadows?' Laurent asked Thérèse one evening. 'Is that why you are shaking? Drowned men do not return from their graves, do they?'

'You know that they do, you murderer!' Thérèse replied. 'You killed him. It is because of you that he comes here.'

'And did you help Camille when I pushed him in the water?' Laurent asked his wife. 'No! If I'm a murderer, then so are you. We both wanted him dead.'

'We were fools!' Thérèse said. 'Our lives were better when Camille was alive. We made love every day and he didn't know. We were happy then. We killed our own happiness when we killed stupid Camille.'

Madame Raquin was horrified. The poor old woman knew the truth at last, but it was too late. She could do nothing. She tried to speak, but she could not. She tried to move her hands, but she could not. Tears ran down her face.

Thérèse and Laurent saw what they had done.

'We must put her into her bed,' Thérèse said. 'Take her out of this room.'

Laurent picked up the old woman. Her bright eyes stared at him.

'Look at me if you want to,' Laurent said. 'Camille is dead. There is nothing that you can do about it now.'

But Thérèse was not so sure. Thursday came and she was very worried.

'My aunt might find a way to tell her friends,' Thérèse told Laurent. 'There's a terrible look in her eyes. I'm sure that she will find a way to tell them our secret.'

'How?' replied Laurent. 'She can't move and she can't

speak. What *can* she do? Nothing! Her friends are stupid. We must behave normally. We are quite safe.'

So that Thursday evening was the same as all the other Thursdays. Suzanne, Olivier, Old Michaud and Grivet sat round the table with them and began to play dominoes. Madame Raquin sat in her chair. She did not move and she did not speak. But she had a plan.

Madame Raquin slowly moved her right hand from her knee. Slowly, very slowly, her hand moved up and onto the table. The hand lay there, soft and white.

'Look at that!' Old Michaud said. 'Madame Raquin can move her fingers! Perhaps she's trying to tell us something.'

The two murderers looked at the hand that was going to tell everyone the truth. One of the fingers on Madame Raquin's right hand moved on the table.

'She is trying to write some words,' Grivet said. 'Yes, she has written your name, Thérèse.' He started to read the words. '*Thérèse and* … Go on, dear Madame, go on.'

Olivier continued reading the message. '*Thérèse and Laurent* … *Thérèse and Laurent are* … ' he said. 'What are they? Your dear children?'

The two murderers were now mad with fear. They almost completed the sentence themselves.

Madame Raquin's hand moved once more and then became still.

'I know what our poor friend wanted to say,' Grivet said. 'Madame Raquin wanted to tell us about her children. She wanted to say: *Thérèse and Laurent are taking good care of me.*'

The others all agreed and they started another game of dominoes.

Madame Raquin was in despair. Her friends had not understood her! Her son's murderers would never be caught and punished[108] now.

———

He started to read the words. 'Thérèse and …'

Two more months passed. Thérèse and Laurent hated each other and they hated their marriage. There was no escape. Their marriage was their punishment and they would never be happy again. Every night, Laurent and Thérèse quarrelled. The guilty lovers made each other angry about nothing. The quarrels started with cruel words and often ended with a beating. Laurent hit Thérèse until he could not lift his fists.

Madame Raquin watched and listened. And so she learnt everything about Laurent and Thérèse's adultery. She learnt about her son's death. Every evening, the old woman heard something new and the tears ran down her face.

Sometimes Thérèse asked Laurent to stop talking about the murder in front of her aunt.

'Let her cry! Who cares about her?' he shouted. 'She can't do anything and we've got her money. We don't have to feel sorry for her!'

And then the quarrel would begin all over again. They did not take Madame Raquin to her own room. She heard every terrible word.

One evening at dinner, Laurent decided that the water in a jug was not cold enough.

'I can't drink warm water. It makes me feel sick,' he said.

'I couldn't get any ice,' Thérèse replied. 'The water tastes all right.'

'No, it doesn't, it tastes like river water,' Laurent told her angrily.

'River water!' Thérèse screamed. 'How can you talk about river water? *You* drowned Camille in the river!'

'You made me do it!' Laurent shouted. 'You sat and watched as I pushed him under the water. You are as guilty as I am. You knew what I was going to do. I told you my plan. Then you got in the boat. You didn't try to stop me, did you?'

'I was too shocked,' Thérèse replied. 'I couldn't think

88

clearly. *You* murdered Camille, not me.'

'You helped me to commit the crime! You are guilty too!' Laurent shouted. 'You asked me to come to your husband's bed. Then you came to my room to make love. You hated Camille and you wanted him dead. You *made* me kill him.'

'The power of your love made me mad and weak,' Thérèse replied. 'I wasn't strong enough to fight you. You've destroyed my life!'

Laurent lifted his hand. He was going to hit her.

'That's right, hit me!' Thérèse screamed. 'Murder *me* too! Then I'll be dead, like Camille!'

And so they went on. They would shout and scream at each other until they could no longer speak. And all the time, Madame Raquin was watching them destroy each other.

Thérèse was on the edge of complete madness. She could not control her thoughts, her feelings, or what she did. The unhappy young woman talked to Madame Raquin for many hours. She told her everything that she thought and felt. She fell onto her knees in front of her aunt and begged her forgiveness[109].

'You were always good to me and I deceived you!' Thérèse cried. 'You can see my pain. Please forgive me!'

Thérèse kissed her aunt and the young woman's tears fell on the old woman's stiff, pale face.

'Yes! You have forgiven me,' Thérèse cried. 'I knew that you would forgive me!'

But Madame Raquin could not forgive Thérèse. She wanted revenge. She wanted the murderers to be punished. That was all that the poor woman thought about.

When Laurent came home, he pulled Thérèse to her feet.

'Get up!' he said to her. 'You are doing this to make me angry. Cry if you want to. But you aren't sorry for anything.'

'I am sorry,' Thérèse cried. 'I'm as guilty as you. I am

guilty of adultery. I am guilty of murder.'

'Well, that's true,' Laurent said. 'But leave the old woman alone. You can see that she hates you.'

'You're wrong. She is good and so was Camille,' Thérèse said. 'I loved Camille and he loved me.'

'If you loved your husband, why did you want a lover?' Laurent shouted.

'I loved Camille,' Thérèse replied. 'I loved him as if he was my brother. Camille and his mother were always kind to me. We were all happy until we met you here. I loved him and I hate you.'

'Be quiet!' Laurent shouted.

'No, I won't be silent!' Thérèse screamed. Tears ran down her face. 'You're a murderer!'

Laurent knocked Thérèse down and held her on the floor. He lifted his hand.

'Hit me! Murder me too!' she cried. 'You're not a man, you're an animal!'

As Laurent hit his wife, Madame Raquin watched and she was happy.

After this, Thérèse began to speak about Camille every day. She spoke about him in every conversation. When he thought about Camille, Laurent became mad and Thérèse knew this. She would repeat Camille's name until Laurent hit her. Then she knew that she had won.

12

Punishment

Madame Raquin's life was terrible. She wanted to die. She decided that she would stop eating. She refused all food. She wanted to kill herself. Thérèse tried to make her aunt eat some food, but the old woman would not open her mouth.

'Leave her alone,' Laurent shouted at his wife. 'If the old woman wants to die, let her die.'

When she heard these words, Madame Raquin made a decision. She did not want to die now. She did not want to make the murderers' lives easier. She decided to live.

Madame Raquin wanted revenge. And she believed that she would not have long to wait. The murderers would soon be punished. Laurent and Thérèse were slowly destroying each other.

Thérèse and Laurent wanted to escape from each other. They wanted to run away, but they could not. If they ran away, their friends would think again about Camille's death. They would remember that Laurent had been Camille's best friend. They would think about how and why Laurent and Thérèse got married. Then they would think that Laurent and Thérèse were guilty of a crime. The murderers would be caught, brought back to Paris, and executed[110].

One day, Thérèse asked Suzanne Michaud to come and serve in the shop with her. Suzanne was delighted and the two women sat behind the counter, talking all day. Madame Raquin and François sat upstairs.

The drapers shop had very few customers now. All the goods were old and dirty. Thérèse did not care about her customers or the business at all. Sometimes she went out in the afternoon and left Suzanne to look after the shop. When Thérèse returned to the Passage du Pont-Neuf in the evening, she looked very tired.

Laurent had nothing to do and he was very bored. He could not paint, because every face that he painted looked like Camille. Sometimes Laurent walked along by the River Seine. Sometimes he slept all day in his studio. The mark left by Camille's teeth on Laurent's neck was still painful. The bite-mark had not disappeared. Laurent saw it every day and remembered how he had murdered Camille.

Laurent hated his wife and he hated Madame Raquin. And his hatred of Madame Raquin's tabby cat, François, became stronger and stronger.

The cat sat on Madame Raquin's knees all day. He watched Laurent with his big green eyes. Laurent began to think that François knew all about the murder of Camille.

One evening, Laurent decided to kill the animal. He picked up the cat and opened the sitting-room window. Immediately, Madame Raquin understood what Laurent was going to do. Two tears ran down her pale face.

François fought Laurent and tried to bite him. But the poor cat could not get away. Laurent threw the animal out of the window. François's head hit the high black wall and, with one terrible cry, he died.

Poor Madame Raquin had cried when her son died. And now she cried when she saw François die.

———

Laurent soon had other things to worry him. Thérèse had became very quiet. She no longer tried to please her aunt. Thérèse also stopped quarrelling with her husband. Sometimes she did not speak to him at all.

Then Thérèse started to go out of the house four or five times a week. Laurent did not trust his wife. He was afraid that she would go the police and tell them about the murder of Camille. He thought that she would confess to the crime. Laurent decided to follow Thérèse and find out what she was doing.

———

Early one morning, Laurent sat down outside a wine-shop near the Passage du Pont-Neuf and waited. After half an hour, Thérèse came out of the arcade. She was dressed in brightly-coloured clothes and her black hair hung about her shoulders. She lifted her dress as she walked and everyone could see her white stockings and black shoes. She smiled at all the men as she walked along.

Laurent followed his wife carefully. She was walking more quickly now. A police officer passed her and Thérèse smiled at him. Laurent was terrified. Thérèse was going to tell the police officer everything! But she walked on until she came to a little café. The tables outside the café were crowded with students and young women. Thérèse sat down at one of the tables and greeted all the young people. The men and women were drinking wine, smoking cigars and kissing each other.

Thérèse spoke to a waiter and ordered a drink. Then she started to talk to a fair-haired young man. When they had finished their drinks, Thérèse and the young man got up and walked away. Thérèse was holding the young man's arm.

Laurent followed them and saw them go into a cheap hotel. A few minutes later, Thérèse and the young man were standing together by an open window. The fair-haired man put his arms round Thérèse and kissed her.

'Thérèse is making love to strangers and they are paying her,' Laurent said to himself. 'I don't care. I'll ask Thérèse for a few thousand francs when she gets home this evening.'

That night, Thérèse came home late. Laurent did not say that he had seen her at the café with the young man.

Thérèse looked tired and she smelt of cigar smoke and wine. She ate nothing at dinner.

'I want you to give me some money,' Laurent said. 'Five thousand francs will be enough.'

Thérèse refused. 'No. You'll soon want more,' she replied. 'We're spending too much money. You've got no job. The shop isn't making any money now. I give you an allowance of one hundred francs a month and I pay for all your food. That's more than enough.'

'I want five thousand francs,' Laurent said again.

'We've bought everything for you for four years!' Thérèse shouted. 'There's a word for a man who women pay for!'

'You've learnt that word from your new friends,' Laurent said. But he did not say more. He did not tell Thérèse that he had seen her with her new friends.

Thérèse looked at her husband with anger in her dark, shining eyes. 'At least my new friends are not murderers,' she said quietly.

Laurent's face became very pale. 'I don't want to quarrel any more,' he said. 'Give me the money.'

'No.'

Laurent jumped up and Thérèse thought that he was going to hit her. 'You're making me mad!' he shouted. 'I shall go to the police and tell them everything.'

Thérèse stood up too. 'Very well,' she said. 'Let's go to the police together.'

'Yes. We'll go together,' Laurent replied.

But when they got downstairs they both stopped. They were too afraid to go any further. Thérèse was the first to speak.

'You can have the money,' she said. 'I don't care.'

She left the room and came back a few minutes later with five thousand francs.

Laurent now had money and he began to enjoy himself.

He went out with women. He got drunk in wine-shops and sometimes he stayed out all night. But nothing made him feel happy. Laurent did not care for food and kisses any more. And when he returned home to Thérèse and Madame Raquin, he felt afraid again. After a few weeks, he decided not to spend any more money.

Then Thérèse stopped going out and meeting men. Nothing made *her* happy now. She stayed in the house, wore dirty clothes and did not wash herself.

The two murderers were together in the house all day. They began to quarrel again. They both said that they would go to the police and confess. They watched each other with fear in their eyes. Thérèse began to wish that Laurent was dead. And Laurent began to wish that Thérèse was dead. Only a second murder could save them.

Laurent decided to kill Thérèse because he hated and feared her. Thérèse decided to kill her husband for the same reasons. Their plans were exactly the same. First, murder, then escape with Thérèse's money. Thérèse had hidden the money, but Laurent knew where it was.

Laurent bought some prussic acid – a powerful poison. Thérèse took a sharp knife from the kitchen and hid it in the pocket of her dress.

Thursday evening arrived and the domino players walked cheerfully up the stairs to the room over the drapers shop. They had been meeting together every Thursday for four years. They had never thought that anything was wrong in the Raquins' home. And they did not think that anything was wrong on this day. They were sure that the Raquins were all happy.

Thérèse and Suzanne talked together, as usual. Grivet told his silly jokes, as usual. Laurent laughed loudly at all of Grivet's stories, as usual.

Madame Raquin waited and watched. Soon the murderers

would be punished for their crime. She hoped that she would live long enough to see them punished.

That evening, the friends stayed much later than usual. It was half past eleven when they finished their last game of dominoes. Grivet and the Michauds got ready to leave.

'This is such a happy place. We never want to go home,' Old Michaud said and he smiled at Madame Raquin.

'I'll be here tomorrow at nine o'clock,' Suzanne said to Thérèse.

'No,' Thérèse said quickly. 'I'll be out tomorrow morning. Come in the afternoon.'

Thérèse and Laurent went downstairs with their visitors and locked the door of the shop. Their hands were shaking and they did not look at each other. Then they went upstairs and sat down at the table. They did not look at Madame Raquin.

Suddenly Laurent said, 'Well, are we going to bed?'

'Yes, we're going to bed,' Thérèse replied. She stood up and picked up the water jug. 'I'll prepare a drink for us before you take aunt to her bed.'

'No. I'll make a drink tonight,' Laurent said quickly. He turned away from his wife and filled a glass with water from the jug. He poured the poison into the glass and then put in some sugar.

As Laurent turned away from her, Thérèse pulled the knife out of her pocket.

They both turned towards each other at the same moment. Thérèse looked at the glass and then Laurent saw the knife in his wife's hand. Madame Raquin sat and watched.

Suddenly, Thérèse and Laurent began to cry. They stood completely still, looking at each other for the last time. Then Thérèse took the glass, drank half of the poisoned water and gave the glass back to Laurent. He drank too.

96

*Thérèse took the glass, drank half of the poisoned water and
gave the glass back to Laurent.*

As they fell down to the floor together, Thérèse's mouth touched the mark on Laurent's neck.

———

Laurent and Thérèse lay on the sitting-room floor all night. The light from the lamp shone down on their twisted bodies.

For almost twelve hours, Madame Raquin stared at the corpses of the murderers. She could not move and she could not cry out. But she had a look of terrible joy in her eyes. She was happy. Her son's murderers had their punishment at last.

Points for Understanding

1

1 How had Madame Raquin spoilt Camille?
2 Describe the differences between Camille and his cousin.

2

1 Why is Thérèse in despair when she sees the drapers shop in the Passage du Pont-Neuf?
2 Who comes to the house every Thursday evening and why do they come?

3

1 How does Thérèse behave when she meets the new visitor?
2 Describe the portrait of Camille.
3 What happens on the evening that the painting is finished?

4

1 Thérèse amazes and frightens Laurent. Find six adjectives which describe how Thérèse has changed.
2 Who frightens Laurent by looking at him with big green eyes?

5

1 Laurent does not sleep after Thérèse visits him in his attic room. Who or what does he think about?
2 Where do Camille, Laurent and Thérèse go at eleven o'clock on one Sunday morning?
3 On the small island, who or what: (a) make a dry crunching noise (b) smells of violets (c) is slim, beautiful and black and white?

6

1 Camille, Laurent and Thérèse look at the boat. Why is Camille
   afraid? Why is Thérèse afraid?
2 What happens to Laurent as he throws Camille into the water?
3 Laurent deceives the young men when he tells them about the
   accident. Laurent tells them, 'As my friend fell into the water,
   he called out, "Help my Thérèse!"' Are these the true words that
   Camille shouted? Explain.
4 (a) Where does Laurent go when he reaches Paris? (b) Why does
   he go to this place? (c) What happens next?

7

1 Why does Laurent have bad dreams for more than a week after
   Camille's death?
2 What happens on the tenth day after Camille's death?
3 Fifteen months after Camille's death some things had changed.
     (a) What has changed for Laurent and how does he feel?
     (b) What has changed for Thérèse and how does she feel?
4 Why does Laurent not trust Thérèse now?

8

1 Look back at the description of the portrait of Camille in
   Chapter 3. What comparison can you make in this chapter?
2 Who suggests that Thérèse and Laurent should marry?

9

1 What terrible mistake does Laurent make on his wedding night?
   What happens next?
2 Why does Laurent want Thérèse to kiss his neck?
3 What does Laurent think he sees in the corner of the room? What
   is it really?
4 What does Laurent think he hears? What is it really?

10

1 Why do Laurent and Thérèse leave a wide space between them
   when they lie on the bed?
2 'But soon Thérèse and Laurent had something different to worry
   about.' What happens?
3 What decision does Laurent make after four months?
4 Why is Laurent's artist friend surprised?
5 Why is Laurent terrified after he meets his friend?

11

1 Madame Raquin has a stroke. How does this illness change her
   life?
2 How does the old woman's illness change Laurent and Thérèse's
   behaviour?
3 Grivet misunderstands Madame Raquin's message. What do you
   think she was trying to say?
4 How do the quarrels between Thérèse and Laurent often end?

12

1 Madame Raquin tries to kill herself. How?
2 What happens to: (a) Francois (b) Laurent (c) Thérèse
   (d) Madame Raquin?
3 Now imagine that you meet the friends who play dominoes. What
   do you think they would say about Thérèse, Laurent and
   Madame Raquin?

Glossary

1 **clerk** (page 4)
a person who looks after documents in an office.
2 **jealousy** (page 5)
a feeling of sadness and anger because someone has something that you want. When someone has something that you want, or does something that you want to do, you feel *jealous*.
3 **affairs** (page 5) sexual relationships.
4 **recognized** – *to recognize* (page 5)
people read Zola's work and they believed that he was one of the very best French writers. The common meaning of *recognize* is: to know a person and remember where you have seen them before.
5 **tradespeople** (page 5)
people who buy and sell goods.
6 **smugglers** (page 5)
people who break a law when they take particular things out of a country, or bring things into a country.
7 **destroyed** – *to be destroyed* (page 5)
when something terrible happens and people's lives are never the same again, they are *destroyed*. Someone's *happiness can be destroyed* if another person is cruel to them, or takes everything away from them.
8 **accused** – *to accuse* (page 6)
say that someone has done something wrong, or broken a law.
9 **crime of spying** (page 6)
a *crime* is when you do something which breaks a law. For example, stealing and murder are crimes. When a person steals something or murders someone, they are *committing the crime* of theft or murder. People who give the enemies of their country information about their own country are spies. They are committing the *crime of spying*.
10 **found guilty** – *to find someone guilty* (page 6)
when someone breaks a law the police take them to a court of law. The judge and the court decide if the person has broken the law and committed that crime.
If the judge and the court decide that the person did break the law, the person is *found guilty*. He or she might have to pay some money or go to prison.

If the judge and the court decide that the person did not break the law, the person is *found not guilty*. The innocent person can then leave the court.

11 **escaped** – *to escape* (page 6)

quickly leave a place where there is danger.

12 **poisonous** (page 6)

poison is a substance that can make a person very ill, or it might kill them. Some plants, animals, chemicals and gases are *poisonous*.

If a poison enters a person's body they could become ill, or even die. As a fire or a stove in a room burns, poisonous gases go into the air. If all the windows and the doors of the room are shut, the room fills with poisonous gases. These gases will kill a person who stays in that closed room.

13 **adultery** (page 6)

if a man and woman have a sexual relationship and one of them is married, they are *committing adultery*.

14 **revenge** (page 6)

do something to someone because they have hurt you, or someone who you know. When you do something to a person who has hurt you, you are *taking revenge*.

15 **Normandy** (page 8)

a northern region of France.

16 **drapers shop** (page 8)

a shop where cloth and things made of cloth are sold. *Drapers shops* might also sell things like buttons, ribbons etc. (See Glossary No. 50.)

17 **rent** – *to rent* (page 8)

pay to live in someone's apartment or their house. The amount of money that you agree to pay every week, month or year, is the *rent*.

18 **bank** (page 8)

the raised area along one edge of a river.

19 **blotchy** (page 8)

having many marks on it.

20 **spoilt** – *to spoil* (page 8)

change someone or something in a bad way. Madame Raquin has always done everything for Camille. She has never made him help her. *Spoilt* people believe that they can have whatever they want, whenever they want it. Spoilt people will not listen to advice.

103

21 **treated** – *to treat someone* (page 8)
look after someone in a special way, perhaps because you believe that they are sick or unhappy.

22 **sickly** (page 8)
unhealthy. Someone who has a lot of illnesses is *sickly*.

23 **weak** (page 8)
not strong. A person can have a *weak mind* or a *weak body*. Someone with a weak body feels ill and cannot walk easily. Someone who does not know what is right or wrong, and cannot make a decision, has a weak mind.

24 **selfish and vain** (page 9)
a *selfish* person only thinks of what they feel or want. Someone who is *vain* thinks that they are good looking and important.

25 **expression** (page 9)
the way that a person's face shows their feelings. Their *expression* shows that they are happy, sad, angry, in love, worried, etc.

26 **sewed** – *to sew* (page 10)
join pieces of cloth together with a long thin thread.

27 **tabby** (page 10)
a cat that has stripes of grey, brown or black fur on its body.

28 **nodded** – *to nod* (page 10)
move your head up and down to show that you agree with someone's words.

29 **fists** (page 12)
when you close your fingers onto your hands, your hands become *fists*. People use their fists to hit each other during a fight.

30 **brave** (page 12)
a *brave* person is strong and does not show fear when they do something which is painful or dangerous.

31 **took no notice of** – *to take no notice* (page 13)
when you look at someone, or you know that someone is near to you, you *notice them*. If you know that someone is near to you, but you do not look at them, you *take no notice* of them.

32 **behaved** – *to behave* (page 13)
the way that you do or say things. A person's *behaviour* can be good or bad.

33 **complained** – *to complain* (page 13)
say that you think something is wrong and that you are unhappy about it. When a person goes to a second person and says that a third person has done something wrong, the first person is making a *complaint* about the third person.

34 **country** (page 13)

the land outside towns, where there are farms, trees, mountains and lakes is called the *countryside*. This word is often shortened to *country*.

35 **arcade** (page 14)

an area or a street which has shops on either side and is covered with a roof.

36 **Passage du Pont-Neuf** (page 14)

a *passage* is a small, narrow street which goes between two larger streets. *Pont* means bridge. *Neuf* means nine.

The Passage du Pont-Neuf = a narrow street near the ninth bridge which crosses the River Seine.

37 **cheaply** (page 14)

the organization did not cost much money to buy.

38 **paved** – *to pave* (page 15)

ground that is covered in large flat pieces of stone is *paved*. The pieces of stone are called *paving*.

39 **cracked** (page 15)

having lines which show that the stones are broken.

40 **lanterns** (page 15)

glass containers with lights inside them. At the time of this story, electricity was not common. Homes and streets were lit by flames of burning gas or oil.

41 **grave** (page 15)

when someone dies, their body is put into a hole in the ground and it is covered with earth. The body is buried in this *grave*. An *open grave* has not been covered with earth.

42 **counter** (page 15)

a long flat surface where customers buy their goods in a shop.

43 **spiral staircase** (page 15)

stairs that curve around a large central post as they go up.

44 **in despair** – *to be in despair* (page 16)

be extremely unhappy.

45 **stiff** (page 16)

Thérèse holds her body straight and does not move.

46 **wallpaper** (page 16)

a thick paper that is stuck onto the walls inside a house. *Wallpaper* might be coloured and it sometimes has patterns or pictures on it.

47 **looked forward** – *to look forward to* (page 16)

think happily about something that will happen in the future.

105

48 **stockings** (page 17)

thin coverings that women wear on their legs.

49 **wool** (page 17)

a soft thick thread that is made from the hair of sheep.

50 **knitting-needles, boxes of buttons and cheap ribbons** (page 17)

knitting-needles are pairs of metal or wooden pins that are used with a wool thread to make soft warm clothes. *Buttons* are small round objects that fasten clothes. Buttons are pushed through holes in the cloth to join the edges of clothes together. Narrow strips of cloth which are used to fasten things together, or decorate clothes are called *ribbons*.

51 **served** – *to serve* (page 17)

sell things to people who come into a shop, cafe or restaurant.

52 **shutters** (page 19)

wooden covers that can be put over windows at night or during bad weather.

53 **dominoes** – *to play dominoes* (page 19)

dominoes are small, flat pieces of wood that have different numbers of spots on them. They are used to *play a game* called *dominoes*. Players try to place each of their dominoes next to another person's domino which has the same number of spots on it.

54 **Police Commissioner** (page 19)

an important police officer who is in charge of a large department of police.

55 **retired** – *to retire* (page 19)

stop working because you are ill or too old.

56 **respected** – *to respect* (page 19)

be very polite to someone because you think that they are clever or important.

57 **headache** (page 20)

a pain in your head.

58 **half-asleep** (page 20)

half is used as a prefix to a word when something happens but it is not complete. Thérèse is not completely asleep and she is not completely awake. She is *half-asleep*.

Other words which can take the prefix *half-* are 'mad' (*half-mad*), and 'dead' (*half-dead*).

59 **real man** (page 23)

Camille is an unattractive, weak man and he never makes love to Thérèse. For the first time, Thérèse sees an attractive, strong man who likes women. She is excited when she sees Laurent.

60 **allowance** (page 23)
an amount of money that a person receives from someone each week, month or year.

61 **refused** – *to refuse* (page 23)
say that you will not do something that someone has asked you to do.

62 **models** (page 23)
men or women who sit or stand in an artist's studio so that the artist can paint pictures of them.

63 **lazy** (page 24)
a *lazy* person will not do anything that is difficult or tiring.

64 **make love** – *to make love* (page 24)
when someone says and does things which show that they are in love with another person, they are *making love to* that person.
Here, this phrase has a stronger meaning. It means: to have sex with someone.
The word *lover* can be used in two ways. Someone who loves another person very much is a *lover*. The word *lover* is also used for a person who has a sexual relationship with someone.

65 **portrait** (page 24)
a painting which shows a person's face.

66 **curl** – *to curl* (page 24)
bend pieces of hair into curved shapes. At this time, both women and men *curled* their hair.

67 **brandy** (page 26)
a strong alcoholic drink made from fruit such as grapes or apples.

68 **easel and paints** (page 26)
an *easel* is a frame which holds the picture while the artist paints or draws it. *Paints* are coloured powders which are mixed with oil. An artist uses paints when he or she paints a picture.

69 **prepared his canvas** – *to prepare the canvas* (page 26)
a piece of cloth is attached to a wooden frame. Then the cloth is covered with a special thin liquid. When the canvas is dry, it becomes hard and flat. The canvas has *been prepared*. The artist can then start painting their picture onto the canvas.

70 **try to seduce** – *to try to seduce* (page 27)
do or say things which will make someone have sex.

71 **twisted** (page 27)
bent into an unusual shape.

72 **drowned** – *to drown* (page 27)
a person who sinks under water and dies, has *drowned*.

107

A person can kill someone by *drowning them* – pushing them under the water until they die.

73 **brutal** (page 28)
very violent.

74 **alley** (page 28)
a narrow street between or behind a building.

75 **petticoats** (page 29)
skirts which were made of white cloth that women wore under their long dresses. At this time, women wore many *petticoats* under their dresses. They made the skirts of their dresses very wide.

76 **violets** (page 29)
small blue flowers with a strong sweet smell.

77 **desire** (page 29)
if you have a *desire* for someone, you want to make love to them. Camille never wants to make love to his wife. He has *no desire* for her.

78 **drunken** (page 29)
a *drunken* person is someone who has drunk so much alcohol that they cannot speak clearly or walk easily. Laurent's feelings for Thérèse are so strong that he walks like a drunken man.

79 **bedclothes** (page 32)
the sheets, blankets and covers on a bed which keep a person warm.

80 **pretended** – *to pretend* (page 32)
speak and behave in a way so people believe that something is true, when it is not.

81 **deceiving** – *to deceive* (page 33)
trick someone or make them look foolish.

82 **skylight** (page 36)
a square window in a roof.

83 **share** – *to share* (page 39)
use or have something at the same time as someone else. You can *share a room*, or *a bed*. If you *share someone's life*, you are with them during difficult times and good times.

84 **unsolved crimes** (page 39)
if the police cannot find out how a crime happened and who did it, the *crime is unsolved*.

85 **traffic** (page 40)
all the people and vehicles that travel in the streets of a village, a town or a city.

108

86 **cab** (page 41)

a vehicle pulled by a horse. Cabs could carry two passengers. In modern usage, *cab* means a taxi.

87 **parasol** (page 41)

a light umbrella which women carried in the summer to keep the sun off their faces.

88 **terrace** (page 43)

an area outside the café where customers can sit to eat their meals. The *terrace* of this café is built above the ground. People can sit at tables on the terrace and can look down onto the river.

89 **boat-trip** (page 44)

a journey on a boat.

90 **hired out** – *to hire out* (page 44)

take money from a person who wants to use something that you own.

91 **rowing-boat** (page 44)

a boat which is pulled through the water – *rowed* – with pairs of *oars* – long pieces of wood which are attached to the sides of the boat.

92 **fainted** – *to faint* (page 47)

suddenly fall to the ground and be unable to see or hear for a short time. People *faint* because they are ill or they have had a shock.

93 **It was my fault!** (page 47)

when you do something which makes a problem or trouble for another person, *it is your fault* that this has happened.

Laurent is being very clever here. He quickly says that he should have looked after Camille more carefully. He pretends to be very upset by what has happened. So all the people on the river believe his words. They never think that he has killed Camille.

94 **omni'ous** (page 48)

an old word for 'bus'. *Omnibuses* did not have engines. They were pulled by two or four horses.

95 **suffering** – *to suffer* (page 49)

feel great pain in your body, or feel great sadness in your mind.

96 **confess** – *to confess* (page 50)

tell people that you have done something wrong or broken a law.

97 **death certificate** (page 52)

an official paper which gives the name of a dead person and says when and how they died.

Death certificates had to be written and signed by an important person such as a doctor or city official.

98 **mirror** (page 55)
   a special piece of glass in which you can see yourself, or something
   which is behind you.

99 **not trust** – *to not trust someone* (page 60)
   believe that someone will say or do something to hurt you.

100 **matches** (page 61)
   small wooden sticks that make a flame when they are rubbed
   against something which is rough.

101 **town hall** (page 71)
   the most important building in a town. An official at the *town
   hall* can say the special words and prepare the official document for
   a marriage between a man and a woman.

102 **marriage ceremony** (page 71)
   special words that a priest or an official speaks when two people get
   married.

103 **disgust** (page 72)
   the feeling that you have when you see, hear, touch or smell
   something that is unpleasant.

104 **spat** – *to spit* (page 75)
   send clear liquid out of your mouth.

105 **scratching noise** (page 75)
   the sound made by an animal when it pulls the sharp claws on its
   feet across wood or stone.

106 *from his imagination* (page 81)
   Laurent paints pictures of the things and people that he sees in his
   mind.

107 **stroke** (page 84)
   if a person's blood cannot reach their brain for a few minutes, they
   suddenly become ill. The illness is called a *stroke*. Someone who
   has had a stroke might never speak or move easily again.

108 **punished** – *to punish* (page 86)
   when someone does something wrong and you make them feel
   sorry, you are *punishing* them.
   A *punishment* is the way in which someone is punished because
   they have done something wrong. The person might be beaten, or
   they might be sent to prison. They might have to pay an amount of
   money, or they might be sent away from their home .

109 **begged her forgiveness** – *to beg her forgiveness* (page 89)
   if someone has made you angry or upset, and then you decide that
   you will no longer be angry with them, you *forgive* them.

110

When someone wants something very much and asks for it again and again, they are *begging*.

110 **executed** – *to be executed* (page 91)
be killed because you have broken an important law. At this time, murderers were *executed*.

Exercises

Korps

Words From The Story 1

Complete the gaps. Use each word in the box once.

> widow dominoes husband colleague kindness portrait
> retired clerk corpse suspected morgue studio guest
> ignore niece stroke wife helpless drapers murder
> invalid artist lovers drowned ghost

---

1 Madame Raquin's husband was dead. Madame Raquin was a
   .... *widow* ....

---

2 Thérèse was the daughter of Madame Raquin's brother.
   Thérèse was Madame Raquin's ..... *niece* ....

---

3 Camille was always ill. His mother called him an ....

---

4 Thérèse married Camille. Camille became her ..... *husband* ..... .

---

5 Madame Raquin's shop sold materials for making clothes. This
   kind of shop was called a ..... *drapers* ..... .

---

6 On Thursday evenings the Raquins played a game. The game is
   played with a set of black tiles. It is called ... *dominoes* ..... .

---

7 Old Michaud used to be a policeman, but he stopped working
   when he was 60 years old. He was a ..... *retired* ..... policemen.

---

8 Laurent worked in the Orléans Railway Company office. He
   worked as a ..... *clerk* ..... .

---

9 Camille worked with Laurent. Laurent was Camille's *colleague*

---

10 Camille brought Laurent to his apartment in the Passage du Pont-
   Neuf every Thursday evening. Laurent was the Raquins' *guest*

---

11 Thérèse did not speak to Laurent. Thérèse pretended to
   ..... *ignore* ..... him.

---

12 Laurent painted a picture of Camille. A picture of a person's
    face is called a .....portrait.

13 Laurent could not paint pictures well. The picture of Camille
    looked like a dead body. It looked like a picture of a ....

14 Soon Thérèse and Laurent were meeting in secret. They had
    sex every afternoon. They were .....lovers.

15 Laurent and Thérèse wanted to kill Camille. They decided to
    .....murder..... him.

16 Laurent pushed Camille into the River Seine. Camille could not
    swim. He sank under the water and died. He .....drowned

17 Everyone believed that Camille's death was an accident. No
    one .....suspected..... that Laurent and Thérèse killed him.

18 The police found Camille's body after ten days. Laurent went to
    look at it in the special place for dead bodies called the city .....morgue

19 Laurent wanted to paint pictures. He wanted to be an .....artist.

20 Laurent rented a room where he painted pictures. He called
    this room his .....studio. .

21 Madame Raquin was unable to move or speak after she suffered
    a .....stroke.

22 Laurent married Thérèse. Thérèse became his .....wife.

23 Laurent and Thérèse believed that they were not alone in their
    room. They believed that the .....corpse..... of Camille was
    with them.

24 Madame Raquin heard Laurent and Thérèse talking about
    Camille's death. She knew that they had killed her son, but she
    was unable to tell anyone. She was completely .....invalid. .

25 Madame Raquin tried to write the word *killers*, but Old Michaud
    thought that she was trying to write the word .....thanks

Making Sentences 1

Rearrange the words to make complete sentences.

> **Example** always had ill Camille been
> ANSWER *Camille had always been ill.*

1 the river went down to Thérèse

_____

2 a mouse is waiting like a cat who looked to catch she

_____

3 to be stupid Camille was boring but the work was too bored

_____

4 customers came but many went people inside few shop past the

_____

·5 had an artist never before the Raquins met

_____

6 an alley from the Raquins' apartment was a back entrance to there

_____

7 to get an excuse Laurent made away from the office

_____

8 Madame Raquin needed her room to lie down in she told Thérèse that

_____

9 had Camille murdered no one that thought been

_____

10 Laurent to have his visits to the morgue because of bad dreams began

_____

Story Outline

Complete the gaps. Use each word in the box once.

> relation found signed building smooth slowly visits
> heart looking sight glass smiling skin wounds horrible
> worried corpse blocks carefully night

sight

The Morgue

Laurent was only [1] .... *worried* .... about one thing.
Camille's body had not been [2] .... *found* .... and so a
death certificate could not be [3] .... *signed* .... If the
body of a dead person was found, it was taken to the Paris Morgue.
The [4] .... *corpse* .... was kept in this cold, damp
[5] .... for several days. People went to the
morgue to see if the dead body of a friend or
[6] .... had been found in a street or the River
Seine. The morgue was a [7] .... place, but
Laurent went there every day.

The dead bodies lay on huge [8] .... of stone,
with cold water running over them. There was a wall of
[9] .... between the corpses and the people who
came to look at them.

Every day Laurent moved [10] .... along the
glass wall. He looked [11] .... at all the bodies,
but he could not see Camille.

Laurent began to have had dreams because of his
[12] .... to the morgue. He went there every day
for more than a week, and every [13] .... he had
dreams. Then, on the tenth day, he saw Camille's body. It was lying
on one of the cold, wet blocks of stone.

When he saw Camille's body, a terrible pain went through Laurent's
[14] .... The drowned man's eyes were open
and he seemed to be [15] .... at his murderer.

115

For more than five minutes, Laurent stared at his dead friend. Camille had been in the water for some time and his corpse was a horrible [16].. . His face was still [17]..., but his [18].. was brown and green. Camille's body had many terrible green and black [19].. on it. His head was twisted to one side and his black lips seemed to be [20].. .

Words From The Story 2

Do the crossword.

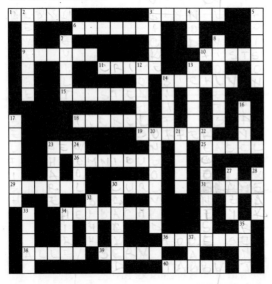

CLUES ACROSS

1A Die from breathing liquid (5)

3A A strong alcoholic drink made from fruit such as grapes or apples (6)

6A A long flat surface where customers buy their goods in a shop (7)

CLUES DOWN

2D Doing something bad to someone because they have hurt you (7)

3D Strong and fearless (5)

4D Move your head up and down (3)

5D A deadly substance, such as Prussic acid (6)

9A To leave a place quickly when there is danger (6)

10A Hands with fingers tightly closed in a ball (5)

11A A serious act of breaking the law (5)

14A Unhealthy. Often ill (6)

15A Bent into an unusual shape (7)

18A Very violent and cruel (6)

19A To feel great pain or sadness (6)

23A To join pieces of cloth together with a thread (3)

25A A frame which holds the picture while the artist paints or draws it (5)

26A An old word for a horse-drawn bus (7)

29A A winding curve – in this story, a kind of staircase (6)

30A Bend pieces of hair into curved shapes (4)

31A A hole in the ground for a dead body (5)

34A A pain in your head (8)

36A Trick someone or make them look foolish (7)

38A A narrow street between or behind buildings (5)

39A Sell things to people who come into a shop, cafe or restaurant (5)

40A A cat that has stripes of grey, brown or black fur on its body (5)

7D Blame or responsibility. When you do something which makes a problem or trouble for another person (5)

8D Small blue flowers with a strong sweet smell (7)

12D People who sit or stand so that an artist can paint pictures of them (6)

13D Say that someone has done something wrong or broken a law (6)

14D Rigid; opposite of supple (5)

16D Cover ground with large flat pieces of stone (4)

17D Thinking only of oneself (7)

20D Unexplained – a crime or a mystery (8)

21D To fall to the ground from illness or shock (5)

22D To see a person or thing and remember you have seen them before (9)

23D Use or have something at the same time as someone else (5)

24D A soft thick thread that is made from the fur of sheep (4)

27D Not liking work or exercise (4)

28D Not strong (4)

30D Having lines that show something is broken (7)

32D The raised side of a river (4)

33D Look after someone because they are sick and give them medicine to get better (5)

34D Pay money to use something for a short time (4)

35D Pay money to live in someone's apartment or house (4)

37D Another word for taxi (3)

Making Sentences 2

Write questions for the answers.

> **Example**   *Where was Thérèse born?*
> ANSWER   Thérèse was born in Algeria.

Q1   *How*
A1   Thérèse was 18 and Camille 20 years old at the start of the story.

Q2   *Why*
A2   They moved to Paris because Camille wanted to go there.

Q3   How
A3   Camille earned 100 francs a month in the railway office.

Q4   Why
A4   Madame Raquin didn't recognise Laurent because she hadn't seen him for years.

Q5   *How*
A5   Thérèse felt bored working in the drapers shop.

Q6   *Which*
A6   The Raquins had guests on Thursdays.

Q7   *What*
A7   They played dominoes.

Q8   *Why*
A8   Thérèse took no notice of Laurent because she was attracted to him and felt afraid.

Q9   *Why*
A9   Laurent came up the back stairs to Thérèse's room so that no one saw him.

Q10   *Why*
A10   Laurent couldn't marry Thérèse because she was already married to Camille.

118

Multiple Choice

Tick the word that is closest in meaning.

Q1 Sickly
    a Poor
    b Unwell ✓
    c Sweetly
    d Impatient

Q2 Plain
    a Unattractive
    b Weak
    c Ugly
    d Blotchy

Q3 Calm
    a Careful
    b Slim
    c Fearful
    d Still

Q4 Cheerful
    a Sad
    b Noisy
    c Happy
    d Welcoming

Q5 Arcade
    a Alley
    b Street
    c Road
    d Highway

Q6 Cheaply
    a Poorly
    b Inexpensively
    c Fairly
    d Reasonably

Q7 Boring
    a Dull
    b Holy
    c Partial
    d Fetching

Q8 Cloth
    a Woollen
    b Lace
    c Material
    d Dress

Q9 Department
    a Flat
    b Office
    c Crossroad
    d Section

Q10 Recognize
    a Understand
    b Feel
    c Know
    d Realise

Q11 Painter
    a Draper
    b Undertaker
    c Decor
    d Artist

Q12 Bell
    a Phone
    b Chime
    c Tone
    d Ring

Published by Macmillan Heinemann ELT
Between Towns Road, Oxford OX4 3PP
Macmillan Heinemann ELT is an imprint of
Macmillan Publishers Limited
Companies and representatives throughout the world
Heinemann is a registered trademark of Harcourt Education, used under licence

ISBN 1–4050–7536–8
EAN 978–1405–075–381

This version of *Thérèse Raquin* by Émile Zola was retold by
Elizabeth Walker for Macmillan Readers
First published by Macmillan 2005
Text © Macmillan Publishers Limited 2005
Design and illustration © Macmillan Publishers Limited 2005

This version first published 2005

Illustrated by Victor Tavares
Cover by Getty Images / The Bridgeman Art Library: Gustave Caillebotte
"Paris, a rainy day" 1876-77.

Printed in Thailand

2009 2008 2007 2006
10 9 8 7 6 5 4 3